ON THE ROAD TO STALINGRAD

MEMOIRS OF A WOMAN MACHINE GUNNER

By Kazimiera J. Cottam

Books

Bolesław Limanowski (1835-1935): A Study in Socialism and Nationalism, 1978

Soviet Airwomen in Combat in World War II, 1983

The Golden-Tressed Soldier, 1983 (Editor and Translator)

In the Sky Above the Front, 1984 (Editor and Translator)

The Girl from Kashin: Soviet Women in Resistance in World War II, 1984 (Editor and Translator)

REVISED EDITION

ON THE ROAD TO STALINGRAD

MEMOIRS OF A WOMAN
MACHINE GUNNER

Z. M. Smirnova-Medvedeva

Edited and Translated by
Kazimiera J. Cottam

NEW MILITARY PUBLISHING
Nepean, Canada

Canadian Cataloguing in Publication Data

Smirnova-Medvedeva, Zoia Matveevna
   On the road to Stalingrad: memoirs of a woman machine gunner

Rev. ed.
Translation of: *Opalennaia iunost'*.
Includes bibliographical references.
ISBN 0-9682702-0-4

   1. Smirnova-Medvedeva, Zoia Matveevna. 2. World War, 1939-
1945. Personal Narratives, Soviet. 3. World War, 1939-1945. Soviet
Union—Participation, Female. I. Cottam, Kazimiera Janina, date. II. Title.

   D811.S59 1997   940.54'81'47   C97-900991-X

Printed and bound in Canada.

NEW MILITARY PUBLISHING
83-21 Midland Crescent
Nepean, ON K2H 8P6
CANADA

Tel. (613) 726-1596
Order Line: 1-888-780-4125

CONTENTS

AS TOLD TO
N. A. KOROTEYEV

TRANSLATOR'S INTRODUCTION

More than 800,000 women served in the Soviet Armed Forces and the Partisans during World War II. They constituted about 8% of the total Soviet military personnel by the end of 1943 and mastered almost every military specialty. Over 100,000 women trained as snipers, and some qualified as machine gunners. For example, the Young Communist League (Komsomol) alone sponsored machine-gun training for about 12,000 women. Women were mobilized for service in the Air Defence Forces, Rear Services, Engineer Troops, and Communications Troops. However, among female Air Force and Ground Forces personnel apparently many were volunteers.[1]

Among such volunteers was Zoya Matveyevna Medvedeva, the author of the original of this book, who fought with the famous 25th Chapayev Division, formed during the Civil War (1918-1921) and decorated with the Order of the Red Banner and the Order of Lenin. During World War II, this Division defended the vital Black Sea ports of Odessa and Sevastopol (5 August—16 October 1941 and 30 October 1941—4 July 1942, respectively). While participating in the defence of these cities, Zoya was also frequently called upon to render first aid instead of, or in addition to, her combat duty, as was typical of many Soviet women soldiers during World War II.

Zoya dreamed of becoming a pilot, and regretted she had been born a girl, having been denied access to a flying club. The club had no need to take girls, since there were already too many male applicants. She was nineteen in 1941. After the war had broken out, she went to a recruitment centre, and was sent to a reserve regiment. She arrived there in July 1941, determined to become a machine gunner (similarly to the brave Anka the Machine Gunner, whose real name was Mariya and who served during the Civil War in the famous Chapayev Division in which Zoya herself was to enlist). Zoya was assigned to a reinforcing company to be dispatched to the front, the sole woman out of 150 male soldiers. After mastering the heavy machine gun in July, she was able to assemble it with her eyes closed.[2] (Unfortunately, I have not been able to find out any more about Zoya's background and native parts.)

Zoya's intent was to write an eyewitness account of the desperate defence of Odessa and Sevastopol, without dwelling on her own exploits, in accordance with the promise she had given to her role model and mentor, the machine gunner Nina Andreyevna Onilova.

In turn, Onilova's role model also was Anka the Machine Gunner, of Civil War fame. An orphan and a former knitted goods factory worker, Onilova was 18 when she volunteered for service at the front. She served in the 54th Razin Regiment of the Division and was decorated twice with the Order of the Red Banner—in December 1941 and February 1942. On 28 February 1942[3] she was mortally wounded in the chest by shrapnel in the fighting near Sevastopol, and the commander of the Independent Maritime Army, the late General of the Army Ivan Yefimovich Petrov (1896-1958), visited her in the hospital while she lay dying. He told her: "Everyone in Sevastopol knows about you, and the entire country will learn about you, too." His prediction came true when the title and Gold Star of Hero of the Soviet Union (the highest Soviet military decoration) were conferred on Onilova posthumously, on the 20th anniversary of Soviet victory over Nazi Germany.

Paying tribute to Nina Onilova, Lieutenant-General T.K. Kolomiyets, former commander of the Chapayev Division/Independent Maritime Army, writes: "After Nina's death, a great many of the nurses who served in the Division kept asking to be transferred to machine-gun duty. We tried to convince them that those who rendered first aid to the wounded, and who often risked death while removing them from the battlefield under enemy fire, were also considered combatants and heroes. All the same, during the relatively quiet periods at the front we organized training in machine-gun firing for a group of nurses, and we made an exception for those who were especially proficient by transferring them to machine-gun duty. Zoya Medvedeva was one of the young women who followed in the footsteps of Nina Onilova.... Moreover, during June [1942] battles, even those young girls who continued to serve as nurses often replaced male machine gunners as they were put out of action."[4]

Since Nina Onilova didn't survive the war, she was not given the opportunity to tell her story. The task was assumed by Zoya Medvedeva, Nina's girlfriend, who had sworn at her graveside to avenge her. This book is a translation of Medvedeva's memoirs: *Opalennaya yunost'* [My Fire-Scorched Youth]. Moscow: Voyennoye izdatel'stvo Ministerstva Oborony SSSR [Voyenizdat], 1967, 152pp.

The late Marshal of the Soviet Union Nikolay Ivanovich Krylov (1903-1972), former chief of staff of the Independent Maritime Army, contributed a foreword to Zoya's next book: *My srazhalis' pod Odessoy* [We Fought for Odessa]. Odessa: Mayak, 1972, pp. 3-5. In the *Foreword*, Krylov recalls permanent strong point No. 1 with its famous machine-gun crew, in the sector defended by the 287th Rifle Regiment/25th Chapayev Rifle Division. On numerous occasions enemy troops tried to capture this pillbox and each time were repulsed by its death-dealing machine-gun fire. He was eventually amazed to learn that Zoya Medvedeva had been commander of this machine-gun crew. (During the defence of Odessa and Sevastopol, he was aware of only two female commanders of machine-gun crews: Nina Onilova and Zoya Medvedeva.)

Krylov gives Zoya a lot of credit for telling her story, in which, in his words, "she describes, with sincerity and authenticity, what she had seen, experienced, and suffered." Assuming that her memoirs would be of great interest to many Soviet readers, he correctly notes that Soviet war memoirs have been written mainly by men: officers, general officers, and admirals. However, he mistakenly believes that Zoya was the sole Soviet female machine gunner to publish a book of war memoirs. V.V. Chudakova, a former machine-gun platoon and company commander, who became a professional writer after the war, had written an auto-biographical book: *Chizhik—ptichka s kharakterom* [The Siskin is a Strong-Willed Bird]. Leningrad: Lenizdat, 1965, 544pp.

This edited translation is a part of my series about Soviet women in combat in World War II. The project was assisted financially by a research grant of the Social Sciences and Humanities Research Council of Canada. It is based on the research which I carried out mainly at the Library of the University of Illinois at Urbana-Champaign. I would like to take this opportunity to thank the staff of this university—both of the Library and the Russian and East European Center—for their assistance, and I am very grateful to Shelley Saywell for her encouragement.

Kazimiera J. Cottam
NEPEAN, CANADA

CHAPTER I

IN THE STEPPE NEAR ODESSA

It was pitch dark. Such darkness is typical of the south on a cloudy late summer night. And drizzling.

We got off the train at Sochi after midnight and went to the harbour immediately. The city and port were swaddled in darkness. Weighed down by it, as it were, we talked almost in whispers, as if our loud talk could violate the blackout. Somewhere beside us, protruding out of the darkness, the crests of the waves shone. They hissed between the black shape of the ship and its berth, beating against them. I knew that there must have been a ship and its berth, but I was guessing rather than actually seeing them in the dark.

Holding onto the kit-bag of the person ahead, we went up the gang-plank which was moving underfoot. On board, to one side of the ladder, stood Lieutenant Ivan Samusev, the commander of our reserve company. On the other side stood the sentry, a seaman. Samusev counted his soldiers as they stepped on board, touching each of them with his hand.

In a single file, still holding onto each other, we went down into the hold. There, side by side lay unfamiliar soldiers. They slept, huddling close to one another, like cartridges in a magazine. Each had a tightly packed kit-bag under his head, and each hugged a rifle. Noting how relaxed the sleeping soldiers were and how they held onto their weapons, I understood that they were not new recruits, even though their greatcoats and footwear were new. Obviously, their unit was returning to the front after regrouping.

We, on the contrary, looked quite different. Our kit-bags were bumpy, packed by inexperienced hands, our greatcoats did not fit too well, and we didn't know how to sleep with our weapons. Frankly, we even had a hard time falling asleep; we kept talking, while Samusev silently paced back and forth along the narrow passage between the prone soldiers, discreetly smoking into his cupped hand.

The hull of the ship kept shuddering slightly, in rhythm with the operating engines. The protracted wail of the siren meant that we were underway. The rolling and pitching increased, and the waves kept hitting the hull with increased persistence, so we knew that we had reached the open sea.

Some of us fell asleep or pretended to be asleep, just as I did. I shut my eyes and told myself mentally that my dream was about to come true. I was going to the front not as a telephone operator, not even as a nurse, but as a genuine soldier—a machine gunner. No one in my company had grounds to consider me inferior in weapons training to any of my male fellow soldiers or claim that allowances were made for me because I was a female. On the contrary, sometimes it seemed that even more was expected of me than of my male comrades.

That phase of my life was now over, and the next day or the day after at the latest I would take up my position behind a machine gun, not on a firing range but in a battle zone. I had a very vague notion what my first battle would be like. Undoubtedly, it was for this reason that I mentally anticipated the future.

Air-raid warnings were being sounded frequently aboard the ship. Someone took a peek through a porthole. I saw that the dawn was already breaking. We heard intermittent aircraft roar. "Stay where you are!" shouted Samusev. With several unfamiliar officers he stood beside the ladder leading to the upper deck. The awakened soldiers looked at each other, confused. The hull of the ship shook from the shells fired by our anti-aircraft guns; Nazi aircraft now roared directly above us. Bullets clicked against the deck and the hull plating of the ship.

It was semi-dark in the hold. The light bulbs gave off a very dim, dreary light. We were in a mood that was just as dreary. Being on a deck during an air raid was not so bad, but sitting in a poorly lit hold was an altogether different matter. Then a distant explosion was heard. "They shot him down! Our anti-aircraft gunners shot down the Nazi!" a rustle travelled through the hold. And even though enemy planes continued to fire their machine guns at the ship, the soldiers in the hold cheered up.

Time passed imperceptibly. The veteran soldiers who lay beside us displayed much less exuberance than we—the new recruits who had never been under fire—did. At first I failed to understand why. It was only later on, when we were nearing our destination, that one of them said: "We got through, after all. We didn't hit a mine and a submarine didn't intercept us." So I finally understood why our fellow passengers were so reserved; they didn't want to frighten us, raw recruits, needlessly.

At the height of another air attack, a middle-aged soldier beside me spat on his fingers, smoothed out his black moustache, and asked in a loud voice: "Why be so quiet, lads? Let's sing! Come what may, a song makes life merrier." No one responded, but he persevered in a warm-hearted fashion: "I'll begin and you'll join in." And then he broke into a song, singing in a surprisingly clear voice:

O black raven! O black raven!
Why do you circle so above me?

Then and there our Anatoliy Samarskiy couldn't resist picking up his accordion and opening its bellows. Apparently, our singing cheered up the anti-aircraft gunners and their guns began to fire faster. Then "All Clear" was sounded.

Then a naval officer went down into the hold saying: "Congratulations on your safe arrival, comrades! Get ready to disembark!" So, stepping out into the darkness of another night, and again holding onto the kit-bag of the person ahead, we ran down the ladder onto the shore. We were in Odessa! We have heard so much about the city's defenders. And now it was up to us, too, to defend the city, fighting alongside them shoulder to shoulder.

Next we marched for almost twenty-four hours along dusty steppe roads. Gloomy, silent refugees advanced toward us along the shoulders, their unmilked cows bellowing in clouds of dust. In the distance ahead of us, black smoke drifted along the horizon; it came from stacks of burning wheat.

Suddenly, a severe looking old man, leading a goat on a string, approached Samusev. "Well, my son, are you going to stop them?!" he demanded. The Lieutenant lost his composure. "We have not seen action yet. We are only on our way...." he answered meekly. "Well then, keep going!" said the stern old man, sounding like a general.

And so we kept marching without pausing for a rest. In the afternoon we passed the burning wheat. Ahead of us, it was now a reddish smoke, smelling of explosives and dust, that drifted along the horizon. And the ground underfoot kept shaking almost imperceptibly, as if it were in pain, from the distant shell explosions.

It was twilight when we entered the village where we expected to meet the guide who would take us to the battle zone. Half of the village had been destroyed by incendiary bombs; all that remained there were smoking ruins. The fire victims could be identified immediately by their blackened faces. They and the refugees congregated in the orchards, under the deceptive shelter of the trees.

I entered one orchard, where women and children were sitting on the ground. The women crushed ears of wheat in the palms of their hands, having gathered them on the way. After blowing off the chaff, they chewed the grain and then fed it to their children. According to my short but bitter military experience, I knew that even cooked wheat—when cooked insufficiently—gave one bad stomach cramps, not to speak of raw grain. Turning to a refugee woman beside me who was feeding this "cud" to her baby, I asked: "What are you doing? That raw grain will make your baby sick!"

Tears rolled down the woman's cheeks. "My dear young girl.... My milk has dried up. I left everything behind—the house, bread, milk, and my man."

I stepped to one side, untied my kit-bag, took out my dry rations, and handed them to the woman. Samusev and the company sergeant major saw what I had done—this was against the regulations—but didn't say anything. They looked the other way, too, when other soldiers also gave away their rations to the children. What's more, they furtively did the same themselves.

Eventually the guide arrived, and we were on our way. The night sky ahead of us lit up with blinding flares and multi-coloured tracer bullets. The dull, muffled sound of a firing heavy machine gun came from the right; shell explosions were also heard. Later on, we learned that what we saw and heard came from the regiment which our reserve company was to reinforce; it had stubbornly fought for several days for a small settlement and a highway crossing.

By the time we reached the disposition of the regiment it was very late. We made a halt. Many of our soldiers, tired out by the long march, immediately fell asleep on the ground, churned up by shells. Eventually, an apparition wearing a white apron and cap materialized before us. It was the cook. Fidgeting with a scoop, he greeted us thus: "Hello, new recruits! You'll get one mess tin for two. Help yourselves to a front-line breakfast."

"Anything good for breakfast?" someone asked in a sleepy voice.

"Rice and lamb pilaff! Taste it and find out for yourselves!"

"Well, if that's the case, it is worth getting up for."

We formed up in a single file and set off for the regimental kitchen. The pilaff tasted so good that we instantly became wide awake. Then Lieutenant Samusev came out of the HQ, accompanied by the commanding officer and senior political instructor. After greeting us the political instructor said: "Even though the pilaff tastes very good, you shouldn't praise it in a loud voice. The Germans are close by and may instantly open fire in the direction of the voices. You've not walked this far to praise the cook and get yourselves killed in the process. This would be out of keeping with the record of our division that was named after Vasiliy Ivanovich Chapayev, the Civil War hero. Our regiment belongs to the division."

Then the political instructor informed us that we were to reinforce a famous company of the regiment, which had been depleted in the course of the latest bloody fighting. For several days, the famous company had been repelling the attacks mounted by the enemy with the aim to break through to the Black Sea via an important arterial road, along which were moving our retreating units, exhausted by fierce engagements, as well as refugees escaping from the occupied territory.

We hastily finished eating our pilaff, got up, and followed the messenger sent from our battalion HQ. I was curious to know how far it was to the battle zone. "A stone's throw from here," was the answer. Yet we walked for at least two hours, tripping and swearing in the dark. "You are lucky," said our guide. But only a few middle-aged soldiers understood what he meant. We were indeed fortunate that the moon was hidden behind the clouds; if the plain across which we were advancing were illuminated by the moon, we couldn't have moved upright.

A cool breeze was blowing. The leaves began to stir in the thinned out forest we were passing through; broken and fire-scorched branches and tree trunks began to creak. Then large drops of sparse rain came down suddenly. We were exhausted and our feet kept getting caught on all the stumps and roots along our way. My helmet seemed to weigh a tonne. Then someone ahead of me said: "We've arrived." The news instantly passed down the line from the battalion messenger in the lead to the soldier who brought up the rear.

Though we arrived at our destination, we still had to make our way through a winding trench, bumping into soldiers who slept there sitting on their hunches with rifles squeezed between the knees. As we passed, behind us quiet conversations were started and matches were struck as soldiers smoked, cupping their hand-rolled cigarettes so as not to give themselves away. Individual words wafted towards me: "Reinforcements.... New recruits...." A soldier inquired whether there was anyone from his home town among us, and another man asked about Odessa, though we didn't see the city after all.

Samusev conversed with the junior political instructor. They both waited for Senior Sergeant Nesterov, the acting company commander since the commander's death, who had gone to inspect the battle outposts.

The rain stopped just as unexpectedly as it had begun. A wind broke up the clouds, and when they floated past the moon their edges shone. In spite of being tired, no one slept. We lay there, with every nerve sensing the enemy we couldn't see.

Then the sentry near me was suddenly alerted, though I hadn't heard anything suspicious among the routine rustles of the night.

"Halt! Who Goes There?"

"Friend."

"You were gone for a long time, Comrade Senior Sergeant," the sentry whispered.

"Why, have the *visitors* arrived?"

"They've arrived long ago. They are waiting for you."

Nesterov (we realized it was he) lightly lifted the sentry by his elbows, swung him around, and deposited him back on the ground, saying: "Thank you for the good news, Alesha! Well then, now you are in trouble!" And Senior Sergeant Nesterov shook his fist in the direction of the German trenches.

Nesterov walked toward Samusev and greeted him, turning over command. Meanwhile, Vanya Nefedov, the messenger who had accompanied Nesterov on his inspection of the battle outposts, sat down beside our Tolya Samarskiy.

"Are you a machine gunner?" asked Nefedov.

"Indeed, I am. Sit down and have a smoke."

"If only I had something to smoke. Leave me some of yours to inhale."

"Then hold the tobacco pouch."

"As to tomorrow... well, today—it's almost morning already—the Nazis are not likely to attack," said Nefedov.

"Why not?"

"I stood under their very noses for about an hour—and heard not a peep out of them. Apparently, they are exhausted and licking their wounds. We felled quite a few of them yesterday. But the night before last they were so bold—there was so much jabbering in their trenches."

"Perhaps they've managed to prepare for today during the night"?

"I doubt it," said Nefedov with conviction. "I've thoroughly studied their habits. I've special accounts to square with the Germans. My village happens to be located nearby—you must have passed through it. Well, my mother and my younger sister and brothers were killed there in the bombing. I'll not surrender a single lump of soil, a single shard of our demolished family cottage to them."

Nefedov went on talking about himself and about the previous day's fighting. Later on, when the dawn broke and I saw the wrecked field in front of our position, I fully understood what kind of fighting had gone on there—the earth was all churned up and not a single blade of grass remained, with burned out German tanks and corpses of enemy soldiers in their grey-green greatcoats strewn across the landscape.

Loud snores woke me up. Getting up I saw that they came from beyond the next bend in the trench, where a middle-aged soldier slept sitting up and hugging his rifle. Samarskiy, our accordion player, kept touching his arm from time to time, quietly saying: "Be quiet, old man! Shsh! Or else you'll wake up the Germans!" The soldier often nodded, as if agreeing with Samarskiy, but didn't wake up. Finally, Anatoliy couldn't stand it any longer and gave him a little push. The soldier chewed with his lips for a while, raised his eyebrows, and opened his eyes slowly.

"Not so loud, old man! Or else the Germans will hear you!"

"They won't, young fellow. They are still sleeping. It's too early. I know what I am talking about." He stretched luxuriously. "I dreamt so many things! I fought in a battle, visited my son on leave, and dropped in on my wife...." He yawned. "I approached my house and knocked twice on the window pane. But Mariya, my wife, refused to open the door. I banged my fist on the window; a shower of glass splinters fell to the floor. My hand was all covered with blood. Finally, Mariya opened the door and came out onto the porch; she held our baby son Ivan in her arms. Ivan must be walking by now, but in my dream I saw him just as he was when I left him. In a blue dress, my favourite one, she stood on the porch, as if rooted to the ground, and looked at me. Tears rolled down her cheeks, and she didn't say anything.... It was then that you woke me up."

"You should try to go back to sleep, Dad; maybe you'll finish dreaming your dream," I advised the middle-aged soldier. He replied: "Why should I finish dreaming a dream in which I was on crutches? Anyway, there is no time!" He took out a piece of dry bread from his kit-bag, chewed it silently for a while, and then gave me an angry look. "Fancy that! Telling me to finish dreaming my dream! I don't want to! Also, the Nazis might well send us a present for breakfast, at any moment."

But it turned out to be a relatively quiet day. Only a single German machine gun kept firing lazily. Nevertheless, for me that day proved to be very troublesome. When personnel lists were collected from the reinforced platoons of our company, Samusev and his deputy, the junior political instructor, found themselves short one machine gunner. Everyone was accounted for, yet one man was missing.

"I am certain we'll soon find a solution to the problem," said the junior political instructor cheerfully.

"I remember now who is missing!" exclaimed Samusev. "Let's call on Nesterov. This is the Senior Sergeant's doing," he told the junior political instructor.

I overheard this conversation; it took place near the soldiers' dugout and the officers didn't lower their voices. After entering the dugout, Samusev looked at me and then turned to Nesterov: "Comrade Senior Sergeant, you are careless in compiling your lists. You don't know your subordinates. If I were you, I would write Zoya's name at the top. She is the only woman among your soldiers." The missing soldier happened to be me.

Nesterov frowned, and in a quiet voice said bluntly and stubbornly: "Comrade Lieutenant, I know my soldiers very well. I purposely didn't write her name down, first or last, because she is—well, a broad. Broads only bring bad luck when they meddle in men's business."

"That's enough!" ordered Samusev.

"May I explain, Comrade Lieutenant?" asked Nesterov dropping his eyes.

"Go ahead."

"Broads... that is, women... make our chaps uncomfortable. You can't even swear in their presence, or...."

"Drop it! Comrade Senior Sergeant, go to my dugout and wait for me there. Tell the junior political instructor to also wait for me at the HQ."

"Yes, Sir!" saluted Nesterov, turned around smartly, and left.

"We didn't complain, Comrade Lieutenant," one of the soldiers began to justify himself. "Our commander is the one who is dissatisfied."

"Well, that's good," said Samusev and turned to me: "I want you, Comrade Corporal, in my HQ in twenty minutes."

I gave a regulation reply, and Samusev left. The soldiers pulled out their cigarettes, which they had extinguished on his arrival, and lit up again, talking quietly. They sighed, recalling the dressing down their energetic commander had received from the Lieutenant. Then I began to get ready for my appearance at Samusev's HQ. Unexpectedly, on a home-made little table before me appeared a shoe brush, a round tin of "Lux" shoe polish (which I haven't seen since the beginning of the war), a mirror, a cloth, a new button for my field shirt, and a bottle of "Lilac" eau-de-cologne. In addition to all this, the resourceful Samarskiy even produced a snow-white piece of cotton fabric from his kit-bag and gave it to me, to enable me to change the dusty undercollar of my field shirt.

It was easy to shine my boots and sew on the button, but I had no idea how I was going to attach the cotton collar without taking off my field shirt. Again, Samarskiy came to my rescue: "Let's go out, chaps, to smoke in the fresh air!"

I was left all alone, and in two minutes was ready to set off for Samusev's HQ. In the end, I could not resist looking into the mirror. I almost didn't recognize myself. My face was black from sunburn, and on my forehead and around the eyes little wrinkles stood out like tiny white threads. Quickly, I put the mirror down on the table and told myself: "Listen, Comrade Corporal, it's time to give up old habits. You've no use for a mirror now. However, after the war it will come handy. Understood?" And I went out.

Outside, Nesterov's section commanders, who had been summoned by him before his conversation with Samusev, were all milling about— almost as if they were waiting for me. The commander of No. 1 section, a dashing lad with a stylishly curled moustache, quipped: "Your platoon commander is bound to be greatly taken with you now."

"Thank you for your interest in my welfare. Good-bye."

"Don't go yet!" joined in Morozov, the grim-looking commander of No. 2 platoon. "You may join any of my three sections. We'll treat you right, and will allow no one to harm you." He said this so earnestly that I got a lump in my throat. I nodded in his direction and walked quickly toward Samusev's dugout. A sentry stopped me at the entrance. It was Andrey Zaytsev. We were trained together, sailed together across the Black Sea, and marched together into the battle zone. He looked at me, reproachfully shook his head, and tried to strike a conversation:

"Wait a moment.... Oh, what a good dressing down the Lieutenant is giving to Nesterov on your account! He is covered with sweat!"

Voices carried from the dugout, but I tried not to listen.

"Do report that I've arrived," I whispered to Zaytsev, hoping that my presence would somehow save Nesterov from further scolding. "Otherwise, I'll go in anyway." I gave Zaytsev a slight push toward the door. But he leapt from the third step down to the first, and in a single motion flung the door open and found himself in the dugout.

"She has arrived—so let her come in," I heard Samusev say. His tone suggested to me that the matter was settled. When I entered, Samusev was dismissing Nesterov. On the way out, he walked past without looking at me. Samusev was silent for a while, thinking something over. As I waited, I examined the dugout. It had dirt floor, dirt walls, and a ceiling made of thin logs. The newspaper covering the table was mutilated on all sides by smokers of hand-rolled cigarettes and above each of the trestle beds were three peg—for submachine guns, grenade pouches and towels.

"This is what we've decided," began Samusev. "You'll temporarily stay here at the HQ with Mariya Ivanova, our medical NCO [non-commissioned officer]." Blood rushed to my face: "May I speak, Comrade Lieutenant"?

"I am listening."

"I can't function as a nurse. I don't know how to dress wounds. I was taught to fire a machine gun."

"No need to get excited. You'll be more comfortable here. And you won't be in the soldiers' way in their dugout. Well?"

"I have no business to be in the commander's dugout. I can do without special amenities. I am a machine gunner, Comrade Lieutenant!"

Silence followed. Samusev wrote down something in a notebook, and the junior political instructor greedily sucked on a thick hand-rolled cigarette.

"Well, what have you decided?" Samusev finally asked.

"I haven't changed my mind. May I go, Comrade Lieutenant?"

"Wait a moment."

The company commander took out a parcel from under a trestle bed and handed it to me. It contained a new submachine gun. Grease-lubricated, disassembled.

"Can you handle it?"

"Yes, Sir!"

I quickly assembled the weapon, while Samusev and the instructor watched me critically. I was told this was to be my personal weapon, and I should leave the rifle in my possession at the HQ.

"Thank you very much!" I exclaimed.

"What! It's not a bag of candy but a weapon, whose owner was killed yesterday in combat," the company commander admonished me. I stood at attention, and said all that was expected of me, adding: "I'll serve my country just as honourably and selflessly as its previous owner did!"

"Very well, Comrade Corporal."

Leaving, I pushed the door open rather forcefully. A loud gasp was heard. Zaytsev stood at the entrance and rubbed his forehead. "I didn't expect...." he whispered.

"You had no business to stand there!"

"Well, I simply.... I wanted to whisper into your ear: 'Better stay at the HQ. It would be more fun for me, too,'" he said with a smile.

"What am I to you—a toy like a record player?" Offended, I set off for the disposition of my machine-gun platoon. As I walked, my resentment dwindled. I recalled how, at the train station before our departure for the front, Zaytsev's mother—a tiny, round-shouldered, and red-eyed woman —kept pacing up and down the platform in the vicinity of the coach door, begging me to safeguard her son (as if this was in my power).

After I reached a bend in the trench, I turned around. Zaytsev still stood at the entrance of the commander's dugout. In his right hand he held a rifle, and with his left one he still pressed a handkerchief to his forehead.

I spent the rest of the day until dark in a log emplacement. Vladimir Miroshnichenko, No. 1 of our machine-gun crew, familiarized me with the battlefield, showing me the reference points by which our Maxim machine gun was ranged. Soon after we returned to the soldiers' dugout, which was lit up by the tiny flame of a wick lamp, the raincape covering the entrance lifted, and an old soldier came in, carrying a thermos.

"I have cooked some soup with meat and butter for you, Chapayev chaps, to help you keep fit and not to be timid!" the old man said. The soldiers greeted the cook, whose name was Ilya Maksimovich Bondarenko, with joy. He was famous not only for his excellent meals served promptly, but also for fighting in the Civil War under Vasiliy Ivanovich Chapayev himself. Miroshnichenko asked the old man to describe his encounters with Chapayev. So the cook, respectfully and affectionately nicknamed Maksimych, cast an appraising look at the new recruits and slowly began telling his story....

The enemy preparatory artillery bombardment started in the early morning. We all were told what being under a hail of fire would be like before our arrival at the front. We also read about this in books. But none of us had ever before experienced anything of the kind. I sat, my face buried in my lap, in a recess hollowed out in the dry, stony soil, feeling like an ant on an anvil that a blind blacksmith was striking with all his strength; he never missed the anvil and each one of his blows narrowly avoided flattening me completely. This hell lasted 40 minutes, each second of which, I was sure, was my last before my head would split open from the deafening din of the explosions. I tried to plug my ears but it was no use.

After the final, single explosion, a "full stop," as it were, placed after the bombardment, I got out of the recess and dove into the log emplacement. Both the platoon commander—Nesterov—and Volodya

Miroshnichenko, No. 1 of our machine-gun crew, were already there. Nesterov stood beside the embrasure. I looked over his shoulder and saw that between our trenches and the Nazi positions a thick, reddish dust and black fumes, the by-products of the explosions, were billowing. You couldn't discern anything else. I approached the machine gun and adjusted the ammunition belt. For some reason, Miroshnichenko placed a clean rag on the floor of the log emplacement; he ripped it up into strips and emptied the remnants of tobacco from his pockets into them. And even though Miroshnichenko knew that when the tobacco had been distributed I refused to claim my share, he nevertheless asked me: "You wouldn't, by chance, have some in your pockets too"?

I had no time to reply. "Fall in on your machine gun!" ordered Nesterov.

We took up our positions. In front of us still hung the curtain of dust and fumes.

Nesterov took a grenade, threw it up into the air, caught it, and said: "I don't like this silence. I am going to take a look."

Then and there, our regimental artillery opened up.

"Obviously, the Germans are attacking!" Nesterov shouted for our benefit.

The dust in front of the embrasure thinned out somewhat and the silhouettes of enemy soldiers became visible.

"Reference point one! Fire long bursts!" ordered Nesterov.

Miroshnichenko bit into his lip, firing one burst after another. To one side of us, another heavy machine gun was firing. A light machine gun fired very close to us too. I could see how an enemy extended line went to ground and then the soldiers retreated to their forming-up position.

The Germans opened up with mortars. The squeals and moans of the mortar bombs reverberated, as if the steppe were an empty room. Apparently, the Nazis had plotted our machine-gun position, for the mortar bombs fell all around the log emplacement, scattering the camouflage branches aside. Earth crumbled between the logs; some of the timbers of the ceiling were dislodged and it was sagging.

"Lower the machine gun into the log emplacement!" screamed Nesterov. We carried out the order. Miroshnichenko unexpectedly lifted a piece of limestone from the floor and began to examine it carefully.

"This is not the time for geology," the platoon commander said, turning around. "Even though you were trained for it for four years! Better pour some water into the cooling jacket of the machine gun."

This was a task for No. 2, so I went to get water from the small tank by the entrance, kept there so that it wouldn't be underfoot. I don't know why Nesterov turned to Miroshnichenko, rather than to me. Perhaps he wanted to protect me from the buzzing shrapnel which flew into the cracks in the ceiling that was falling apart. Only his concern was misplaced; a shell splinter could have reached me in any corner of the log emplacement.

"Yes," said Miroshnichenko to no one in particular. "I was taught to find treasures in the ground. Instead I am burying in it like a groundhog, lying in wait for enemy troops to help finish them off soon, so that I may return to my proper task."

"Lift the machine gun! They are coming!" ordered Nesterov.

We grabbed the Maxim and placed it back in the embrasure. There was less dust and fumes after the bombardment was finished. I immediately noticed a wild rose bush about 200 metres from the log emplacement, and some distance beyond it I could see enemy infantrymen.

The order to fire didn't come. Apparently, Nesterov was letting the Nazis come closer so we could improve our aim. Miroshnichenko's fingers kept touching the safety catch of the firing lever from time to time, and then he stuck his hands deep into the pockets of his pants, looking at the field ahead of us through the embrasure.

"One of us is lucky," he said, without taking his eyes off the field, along which German soldiers were approaching us.

"Why?" I asked.

"Two such bombardments... The Nazis obviously aimed at our log emplacement and didn't score a single direct hit," said Miroshnichenko. Suddenly, a worried look crossed his face. I, too, glanced through the embrasure. Our reference point—the wild rose bush—was missing.

"Our artillery men and their observers did a fine job!" yelled Nesterov. "They spotted the German machine-gun crew who took up their position by the rose bush, under the cover of their own mortar fire. Our artillery destroyed the machine gun. Everything is OK now!"

The Germans were still quite far away. They either crawled or advanced by short bounds.

Nesterov stayed close to the embrasure.

"The Germans are approaching the second reference point!" said Miroshnichenko, alarmed.

Nesterov didn't reply.

The voices of the screaming Nazis were clearly audible. Nesterov turned around, fixing his long, steady gaze on Miroshnichenko, and suddenly waved his hand and shouted: "Short bursts—fire!"

Other heavy machine guns followed ours, then light machine guns joined in, and rifle shots were heard through their rattle. Other machine gunners were firing short bursts like us, selecting targets and saving ammunition. Then it became quiet on the right flank. It was obvious that our resistance in that sector had been overcome. Suddenly, Nesterov grabbed a submachine gun, pressed himself against the alternate embrasure, and fired almost point-blank at the Nazis who had stolen up toward our log emplacement from the right. A few seconds later he grabbed his shoulder and lowered himself to the floor; blood oozed between his fingers. In the semi-darkness of the log emplacement it seemed almost black.

We heard explosions of hand grenades and submachine-gun bursts; the Germans were very close. We used up so much ammunition that I was already replacing the fourth ammunition belt, but the Nazis had gone berserk, as it were, and still kept pressing forward directly into the path of our fire. Eventually, I found a moment to dress Nesterov's wound. He was already very pale, having lost a great deal of blood. When I returned to the machine gun, steam escaped from its cooling jacket, filling the embrasure. I dashed toward the water tank; it was empty, having been pierced by a shell splinter.

To the right, quite near us, three hand grenades came crushing down. Using his good arm, Nesterov managed to grab his grenade pouch and leaped into the trench. I looked through the right-hand, alternate embrasure and saw that the Germans had driven back our troops on the right flank, captured several trenches, and were about to gain our rear. Nesterov beat them off with his grenades. Then we had a quiet moment, so Miroshnichenko ordered me to render first aid to the wounded in the trench.

I went out and immediately came across Nesterov. He had slipped down to the bottom of the trench and lay there unconscious. Groping in semi-darkness, I grabbed Nesterov under his armpits and dragged him back into the log emplacement. Then I went out again. The winding trench was half-buried in many places and the soldiers who had defended it were all dead. After reaching the second bend, I saw a soldier lying chest against the parapet, with his legs hanging over the trench and trickling blood. I lowered him into the trench, and dressed his wounds. Judging by his location, I figured it was he who had frustrated the first Nazi attempt to capture our log emplacement, and Nesterov foiled the second one. While I dressed his wounds, the soldier regained consciousness, tried to smile, and said with a pronounced Georgian accent: "So you're a nurse too, after all!" Exhausted by his attempt to joke, the soldier lost consciousness again, and I dragged him away, closer to the log emplacement, in order to keep an eye on him.

Afterwards, I continued advancing along the trench, carefully stepping over the corpses in my way. Sometimes I encountered familiar faces, and sometimes I turned over those who lay in unnatural positions....

Beyond the fourth bend I ran into Usov. He sat at the bottom of the trench and was charging the drum magazine of a light machine gun. Nearby, I saw another machine gun and an anti-tank rifle; and beside Usov's feet lay a submachine gun. "You got through, after all," Usov blurted out. "I was sure that you would come to check on me. You couldn't have done otherwise. All sorts of things may have happened to me. Only I haven't received even a single scratch."

At first I couldn't grasp why Usov expected me to come. Afterwards I remembered how, before he was dispatched to the front, he often cried unashamedly, insisting that he would be killed in his first engagement. However, his first bloody engagement had come and gone and Usov was cured of his fear. Despite the situation, he even looked more cheerful than usual.

"How are you coping, all by yourself, with two machine guns, an anti-tank rifle, and a submachine gun?"

"I waited for you for so long," interrupted Usov. "I began to think that something had happened to you. But you made it, after all. How am I coping? I fire the first machine gun, then the second one, then the submachine gun, and then the third machine gun."

"The third machine gun?"

"Here it is," Usov nodded in the direction of a machine gun covered by a greatcoat that was pierced through by shrapnel. "I keep running from one to the other and firing, and that's that."

German bombers appeared over our positions. They began to form up into a circle, each behind the other's tail unit.

"They are going to give us a thrashing," said Usov in a stern voice. "Go back to your log emplacement. There is not enough room for the two of us in this recess."

I barely had sufficient time to reach the log emplacement, or more accurately, the recess beside it, when the first howling Junkers began to attack our positions. I looked up, though I knew I shouldn't have done it.

When you heard an enemy shell whistling or a mortar bomb howling, it always seemed they were about to hit very near you. In fact, when you heard them, they missed you. Similarly, when you saw a plane dive, you thought it was diving at you. Afterwards, you realized the bombs were bound to fall to one side. In both cases, your senses couldn't be trusted.

The explosions blew up the ground with such a force that the limestone in which our trenches were dug out cracked and crumbled, releasing clouds of dust. It became difficult to breathe. Trying to protect my eyes, I curled up in a ball, with my face buried in my lap. I don't know whether it was for an hour or a few minutes that the earth shook, screeched, and shuddered under the Nazi bombs. Suddenly, I heard muffled voices:

"Must be here, somewhere...."

"Right. Here she is under the earth!"

I opened my eyes. Everything was dark. I realized, but not immediately, that I had been buried. I jerked into motion and shouted: "Here I am; here!" I pushed off the earth with one elbow as forcefully as I could. For a moment I saw a spot of light and then I was covered again. However, soon Miroshnichenko and Samusev pulled me from the recess by my elbows.

"She is alive and in one piece!" said Samusev with a smile, cheerful and smart-looking as usual. It even seemed to me that there was less dust on him than on the others. "Back to your machine gun, both of you. I am going to inspect the right flank."

"Comrade Lieutenant, I saw Usov before the bombing; he is doing fine!"

"Thank you, Comrade Medvedeva, for the information. But I want to find out everything for myself."

Here is what happened on the right flank of our company. Even though the night before we tried very hard to approach the battle zone quietly, the Germans apparently noticed some movement in our trenches, and came to the appropriate conclusions. Throughout the following day—the quiet one—they carefully observed our positions. Now, in retrospect, it seems obvious that even an ordinary German soldier could easily have told, on the basis of his observations, that enemy reinforcements had arrived. No doubt, it was also possible for him to guess that these reinforcements were raw recruits. Experienced, battle-hardened soldiers are careful about preparing for the upcoming battle; they don't talk too much and don't wander about in their trenches needlessly, as we did.

So the German commander came to the right conclusion that our side had just been reinforced, probably with new recruits, who therefore were hardly likely to put up stubborn resistance. It is also likely that the Germans correctly guessed the location of the boundary between the flanking company and ours. Perhaps their offensive was planned on the basis of these very data. Thus the Nazis spared no effort to break through to the section of the highway and the village located closest to the area defended by our company. And the boundary between the companies—our right flank—happened to lie on the axis of their main thrust.

After the artillery preparatory fire and mortar bombardment, the Germans hurled themselves into an all-out attack, and it was on the right flank that they came closest to our positions. Then, during the bombing, their fire was again concentrated on the boundary between the companies. As a result, the commander of our right flank platoon suf-fered a concussion. During the subsequent mortar bombardment, his machine gun and its crew were also put out of action.

Of the platoon, thirteen soldiers survived, four of whom were slightly wounded. A new attack began, but of the thirteen no one was willing to assume command and lead the men. The junior political instructor whom Samusev had sent to the right flank at the very beginning of the battle lay severely wounded in a dugout beside the concussed platoon commander. Masha Ivanova, the medic, had stayed behind to look after them. When the Germans approached our positions, throwing hand grenades, the thirteen soldiers began to retreat, forgetting in their haste about Ivanova and the severely wounded officers.

Then the Nazis captured the trenches. They attempted to break through to the rear via the communication trench, but here Ivanova met them with hand grenades. Beyond the bend of the communication trench it was not possible to see that the onslaught was being repelled by a single female medic, who was dragging two severely wounded men to boot.

At that very moment Lieutenant Samusev happened to arrive on the scene. "Halt!" he shouted in the direction of the retreating soldiers. "Chapayev's men don't fight like this!" So the soldiers stopped and look-ed at each other, bewildered. Undoubtedly, they were truly amazed when they realized what had happened. Perhaps each of them believed he had been the only one to falter for a few moments; perhaps he had the urgent need to swallow a bit of fresh air—air that was not saturated with fumes—and to recover from the ear-splitting thunder of the explosions.

However, should one of them shouted "Halt! Turn Back! Expel the Nazis from the trenches!" they would have followed him immediately, just as they were ready to follow Samusev.

"Whom did you leave behind?" asked Samusev.

And the soldiers again exchanged glances. It had not occurred to them that Ivanova remained in the dugout, caring for the wounded. They assumed that the medic had removed the junior political instructor and platoon commander to safety long ago.

"Follow me!" ordered Samusev laconically, waving his pistol. "Arm your grenades!" And the handful of soldiers charged through the communication trench into the trenches captured by the Germans. Anxious to expiate their guilt, the soldiers fought desperately and mercilessly. Only a few of the Germans managed to leap over the parapet and escape.

"Hang on!" said Samusev after the skirmish. "For the time being, I can't promise you reinforcements; you must hang on." Then the Lieutenant appointed the man in charge from among the soldiers and returned to our log emplacement. Just in time.

I had just covered the cooling jacket of the machine gun with a raincape, to protect it from dust and prevent jamming during firing, when a mortar bomb plopped down beside our split roof and something hot splashed on my face. At first I screwed up my eyes; then I rubbed them and realized that my hands were covered with blood and dirt. I looked at Miroshnichenko, and saw that blood was streaming from his head.

"Bandages, quickly!" yelled Nesterov.

I looked at him through my tears; he too was splashed, all over, with Miroshnichenko's blood. Nesterov gave up as hopeless and turned away; then he wiped his face with the sleeve of his good arm—perhaps he rubbed off the blood, or perhaps there were tears on his face.... For two months he had fought shoulder to shoulder with Vladimir Miroshnichenko, a young man who came so close to realizing his dream....

I sat on the floor, confused, and couldn't decide what to do. Should I take the raincape off the machine gun and cover Miroshnichenko's body with it immediately, or wait until the bombardment was over?

"Zoya!" Nesterov touched my shoulder. Apparently, he had spoken to me earlier, but I didn't hear him. "Zoya! Let's put the machine gun in its place!" The two of us—Nesterov could use only one arm—lifted the Maxim. Just then Samusev, out of breath, ran into the log emplacement and helped us.

"They are coming!" shouted the Lieutenant. "They're near!" The voice of the company commander sounded very loud; the mortar attack ceased and it became so quiet that we heard the Nazis screaming. Again I carried out the functions of No. 2, and Samusev assumed the duties of No. 1.

"We must wait a little," he said, placing his finger on the firing lever. "We must wait.... We must wait...." he kept repeating.

So we waited.

We could already distinguish the faces of the enemy soldiers, but still Samusev waited. I understood why he became No. 1; he wanted to give me a lesson in self-control. I also understood that this was the last attack. The sun was already beginning to set and shone into our eyes. The shadows of the Nazis attacking us stretched halfway across the field, and almost reached the log emplacement.

"We must wait...." This was said by Samusev almost inaudibly. To himself, most likely.

I kept looking over his shoulder. When the shadows crept up onto the log emplacement, I saw the huge eyes of the Nazis, made horrible by the fear of death written on them, as they marched toward our silent machine gun. Then the machine gun came to life. Samusev fired a long burst, using up almost half of an ammunition belt. He was an excellent shot. The few surviving Germans went to ground and began to crawl away, while Samusev continued to spray them with short bursts.

"This is to pay you for Volodya Miroshnichenko!" Nesterov kept saying.

Then silence re-established itself on the battlefield. "That's all," said Samusev, tired, and passed the back of his hand under his nose like a little boy. "I daresay, they will not come back here today. But I am worried about the right flank...."

I wasn't sure whether Samusev was talking to anyone of us, or thinking aloud. Then I noticed that Nesterov was shaking his head in a strange manner. No doubt, he suffered a concussion during the mortar attack.

"You must go there," ended Samusev.

"Where, Comrade Lieutenant?" asked Nesterov. He too believed that the Lieutenant had been merely thinking aloud, and he missed what Samusev had said.

"The right flank. You, Nesterov, go on alone for the time being, and I'll send someone to help Medvedeva."

After collecting the remaining ammunition into two boxes, Nesterov picked them up and left. Then Samarskiy lowered himself into the log emplacement. He was wounded in one arm, and was very pale from loss of blood. Nevertheless, he helped me. Without him, I couldn't have coped with the machine gun which at first had to be dragged along the narrow and winding trench. The Maxim became stuck, so I separated the body from the mount. But even then it was not easy to transport it. We had to climb out onto the surface and to negotiate about 50 metres by a quick bound. We were saved by the fact that the Nazis didn't expect such daring on our part, and by the time they fired at us it was too late. All the same, a bullet managed to scratch Samarskiy.

Contrary to Samusev's belief, however, the Germans began their new attack on the left flank. After joining Nesterov on the right flank, we merely began setting up the machine gun when Nesterov was ordered to go back to the left flank. This happened so fast that I had no time to ask him where he had put the ammunition boxes. While I was dressing Samarskiy's wound, I decided that I must get through to Nesterov and ask him about the boxes. Samarskiy agreed, adding: "Otherwise, it would take us a long time to find them, and we don't know where to look."

I left Samarskiy with Maksimych the cook, who had armed himself with a submachine gun. Except for the two men, our right flank was now completely deserted. "Don't worry about the Maxim; I'll take good care of my namesake," the cook called out to me as I was leaving.

I didn't quite reach the left flank. Near our log emplacement I saw Nesterov, along with several wounded soldiers, deliver submachine-gun and rifle fire on a flank of the advancing German infantry. While counter-attacking together with the remnants of No. 1 platoon, Nesterov was wounded in both legs. By then wounded three times, the half-conscious Senior Sergeant nevertheless continued to crawl forward, in the direction where the enemy happened to have been a few minutes earlier, leaning on one elbow and leaving traces of blood on the dusty ground and dry leaves.

When I managed to get across to Nesterov, he was already un-conscious. I applied tourniquets to both his legs, dressed his wounds, and dragged him away into the trench. Here he regained consciousness, looked around with a wild expression on his face, as if trying to orientate himself, and whispered: "Chapayev men! Follow me! Hurry! Hurry!" I bent over the wounded man to calm him down, but when he saw my silhouette he lifted his pistol and fired. The bullet struck my helmet and knocked it off my head.

Dumbfounded and shaking, I remained standing beside Nesterov, who had blacked out again, until Masha Ivanova ran up to me, asking:

"What has happened? Who fired the shot?" After inspecting the wounded man, Ivanova got up and started to scold me: "How stupid of you to leave a weapon in the hands of a wounded man! He regains consciousness and he fancies that he is still advancing toward the enemy. So he mistook you for a German."

Continuing to shake, I replied: "In my haste, I didn't notice the weapon. What's more, how could I have known that he would use it?"

"No need to get upset," Ivanova said kindly. "And don't be angry at the lad. He is unconscious."

"I am not angry. Only he frightened me so." Ivanova patted me on the back: "Here is a handkerchief. Wipe your tears off. And let's go to tend the wounded."

"I must go back to my machine gun."

"There are a lot of wounded. I already had spoken to the Lieutenant. He sent Zaytsev to take care of the machine gun."

After wiping my tears with a piece of bandage, I set off for the dugout with the wounded.

Under the cover of the night the wounded, including Samarskiy, were transported to the medical battalion. Then we buried the dead. Carefully, as if they could still feel pain, we lifted them toward the shallow common grave. It was shallow because only a few of us survived and it was very difficult to hollow out the stony soil. I saw Vanya Nefedov among the dead and realized he will be buried beside an old, tall acacia which, I remembered, he had called his observation post. He had said that his family cottage could be seen from that acacia.

When everyone had gathered, Samusev stepped forward and said: "All of you fought and died like heroes. We stopped the enemy troops in our sector today; we didn't let them come a single step closer to our beautiful Odessa. Let us swear, comrades, that we'll never forget the names of our fallen friends, and we'll fight just like they did!"

"We so swear!" the troops replied in unison, their response reverberating.

Before I was able to return to the wounded in the dugout, Zaytsev came to get me. He explained that Samusev had given him an order that I was to accompany the two of them on an inspection of sentry posts; I was to look for the wounded in the platoons, and if I found any I was to render them first aid.

It was twilight. Usually, the enemy quieted down as soon as it got dark, but that night the Nazis were restless. From time to time shells exploded on our side of the front line. A loud conversation came from the

German trenches. Walking in the lead, Samusev kept stopping periodically and listening for some time to the alarming sounds of the night.

We were making our way along a sparse forest strip, with trees
uprooted by shells and bombs, when a shot rang out nearby and a sentry
challenged us:

"Halt! Who Goes There?"

"Friends," replied Samusev.

"Halt! Or I'll Shoot! Password?"

The Lieutenant gave the password, although we couldn't see the
sentry. We advanced a few more steps. Suddenly, Zaytsev almost tripped over a soldier sitting on the butt end of a log.

"Are you wounded?" asked the Lieutenant.

"Yes, Sir. In the arm and leg. That's why I am sitting down."

The soldier opened his raincape; his bandage was clearly visible in
the dark. "I've camouflaged the wound. What's more, I've a pair of hand
grenades. Just in case. I can't walk; it won't do to face the enemy unarmed! And grenades are handier at night; the Nazis keep snooping all
around."

"Why haven't you been relieved till now?"

"They promised to replace me, but for some reason no one came."

I bent down to help the soldier get up. Then a blinding ball rolled before my eyes, and I was thrown to one side.

I came to in a hospital. It turned out that I was concussed by an
explosion of a German hand grenade. Apparently, it was flung by one of
the Nazi scouts who had broken through to the rear of our company.
From my acquaintances among the soldiers, I learned that Samusev and
Zaytsev had survived, but the wounded sentry with whom Samusev had
talked was killed.

CHAPTER II

BY THE WALLS OF SEVASTOPOL

It was December and the weather was bad. Again I was on my way to the front, on board a ship sailing on the Black Sea at night, but this time it was Sevastopol that we were approaching. On the deck I happened to meet Anatoliy Samarskiy, who was also returning to the front from a hospital. We were as yet unaware then that we would be given the opportunity to rejoin the ranks of the glorious Chapayev Division. Samarskiy was luckier than I; he immediately set off for the battle zone, while I had to stay behind to work in the underground hospital located in the Inkerman Caves[5], near Sevastopol. Fortunately, not for very long. Very soon I managed to persuade my superiors to transfer me to the battle zone.

My first night in Sevastopol passed relatively uneventfully. Enemy bombers virtually stayed away. Low, grey clouds drifted from the sea and a lot of snow fell by morning. The city resembled a soldier in a white camouflage robe. (Incidentally, isn't the purpose of a soldier's camouflage robe to deceive the enemy troops and to mislead them?) At first glance, Sevastopol looked deserted and lifeless. This was how the city appeared to the Nazi observers and pilots. But it rose to the occasion during moments of danger, exerting tremendous efforts and mustering enormous strength. Fire issued from each and every rock, and each hillock became a permanent strong point.

The enemy hung about the walls of Sevastopol, astonished at the bravery and energy of its defenders. But those who lived in Sevastopol at the time, even those who spent there only a few hours, were not astonished. Thin smoke issued cautiously from under the ruins, from dugouts and covered trenches, and looping pathways stretched from one former street to another. The city was alive; it struggled and had no intention to surrender.

One greyish morning a truck going my way brought me to the HQ of my battalion. Here I learned that Samusev was still in command of our company. On my way to the company disposition, passing through a deep communication trench, I literally bumped into Zaytsev, the very same Andrey Zaytsev who, together with Samusev, had been inspecting sentry posts just before I was concussed near Odessa.

At first I didn't recognize him and we almost passed each other by. He advanced bent over, and I only saw his helmet and junior sergeant's collar tabs. Curious, I leaned over these bright, new home-made collar tabs and recognized Zaytsev's snub-nosed face. But he paid no attention to me whatsoever, as if he were passing a soldier with whom he had talked in a dugout only five minutes earlier.

"Just you wait," I thought. "I am going to scare you."

I stood at attention and saluted Zaytsev, my hand touching my cap with ear flaps. I was so excited that I forgot the regulation formula and failed to address him properly. "Greetings to you, Comrade Junior Sergeant!" I said. Then and there Zaytsev almost sat down from surprise.

"Oh, Zoya," he said, shaking his head. "I wouldn't have budged if a German shell were to explode nearby, but you made me shake at the knees."

"Was it your promotion that made you so nervous? After all, you're now responsible for an entire section."

"No, Comrade Medvedeva, this is not the reason. By coincidence, I sent a letter to my mother yesterday, in which I had to justify myself to her on account of you."

"On account of me?"

"Fancy that, on account of you."

"What has come over you, Comrade Junior Sergeant; stop that nonsense! What harm have I done and to whom?"

"Not you, but me."

"Now, this is getting more and more complicated!"

"I had to justify myself to my own mother."

"Well, why, for heaven's sake?"

"My mother is an old-fashioned, religious woman. She told me that I am supposedly immune to bullets and shells, because a guardian angel is watching over me at her request."

"Who is this 'angel?'"

"You, Zoya."

"Haven't you yet recovered from the black eye I had given you with the door of Samusev's dugout?" I asked spitefully, recalling how Zaytsev wanted me to stay at the HQ under his care.

"I did explain to my mother...."

"About the black eye?"

"Of course, not! I told her that we had failed to safeguard Zoya, our guardian angel, and she was seriously concussed in the very first battle.

Afterwards, she was hospitalized in the rear and I don't even know whether I'll ever see her again."

"I still don't understand what you are getting at!"

"And suddenly—you are here!"

"All right, Zaytsev, too bad we are no longer equal in rank; otherwise, I would have told you a thing or two."

"No, no," said Zaytsev, blinking. "You mustn't. After all, it is up to me as the commander of my section to make sure that my men and the entire company are spared the shock of meeting you unexpectedly. Just like the one I've received."

"Quit kidding me!"

"But I am not kidding you. The men remember you, so I'll warn them that you've arrived. And as for you, Comrade Medvedeva, follow me."

It is difficult for me to describe how happy I was to return to my unit and to be reunited with my former comrades-in-arms! Especially when I learned that several of my close friends were still safe and sound. Alas, I was not fated to be reunited with some of them; war is war.... But for a while our reunion made us happy like little children. After all, we were then still very young.... What's more, Maksimych, the old veteran of our Chapayev Division, embraced and kissed me three times. "I feel as if reunited with my own granddaughter, whose name is also Zoya," said the old man, touched.

After the official introductions, Samusev slapped me on the shoulder, saying: "You gave me quite a scare then, Medvedeva! But I see that you've recovered."

"I did, Comrade Lieutenant. I am even more fit than before."

"You are very fortunate, Medvedeva!"

"Indeed, I am."

"I meant that once again you've arrived just in time for the fighting to heat up. We were warned that the Nazis were preparing to storm the city. Their storm has been scheduled for tomorrow. You'll help Ivanova."

Just before the fierce fighting for Sevastopol started, we were admitted into the Komsomol [Young Communist League—Trans.]. The distribution of the membership cards took place in the dugout of the HQ defence platoon. In front of a little table covered with a red cloth, political instructor Sergeyev, who was our regimental Komsomol Organizer, handed out the cards and subsequently shook our hands firmly. In turn, we promised him to spare no effort in defending Sevastopol and, if necessary, sacrifice our very lives.

The next morning was truly terrible. After several hours of uninterrupted aerial bombing as well as artillery and mortar bombardment, the snow in the battle zone disappeared, as it were; the earth had turned black. As soon as the Nazi artillery quieted down, our soldiers came out of their shelters. "Well done!" Zaytsev yelled at them from the trench. "You had the sense to guess what to do on your own; it's time you did."

"It wasn't a hard guess!" retorted Vasiliy Titov. I had just been introduced to this thickset, well-knit soldier the previous day. His comrades told me that a few days earlier he had especially distinguished himself in hand-to-hand combat. Having split his rifle butt against an enemy's helmet, he subsequently fought with his fists until he was able to capture a German weapon.

The German offensive began. Our Chapayev troops met the enemy with rifle and machine-gun fire already on the distant approaches to the city. Since the Nazis intended to take Sevastopol by storm, our troops were forbidden to allow them come too close. There weren't many defenders left in the city, and the fewer Germans approached our trenches the better.

The waves of enemy soldiers kept coming, one after another. The Nazis stealed up by short bounds, advancing from shell hole to shell hole, bush to bush, and tree to tree, and firing long submachine-gun bursts. They were apparently determined to capture the tactical line at all costs.

Deafened by the din of the explosions, Samusev's men kept firing furiously with their miraculously preserved machine guns. The enemy soldiers kept falling to the ground and were being replaced by more and more soldiers. The Germans were about 30 metres away when our Chapayev troops resorted to throwing hand grenades. But, prompted by their squealing officers, the grey-green silhouettes of German soldiers continued to advance toward our trenches, metre after metre.

Dressing a soldier's wound, at first I didn't notice—on account of the noise of the fire and the frequent explosions of hand grenades—that Samusev and his troops were engaging in hand-to-hand fighting. "Hurrah!" rolled along the trenches. Our machine guns ceased firing. I saw Titov running beside Samusev. He apparently noticed a lanky Nazi officer who was firing from behind the trunk of the nearest tree. Titov rushed at him; no doubt, he wanted to take him alive. They both fell, rolling over; now Titov happened to be on top and now the Nazi. Then the German managed to hit Titov on the head with his parabellum gun; apparently, the officer had exhausted his ammunition. Our stalwart fellow let go, and the officer raised his dirk in an attempt to stab Titov. However, Vasiliy

Kozhevnikov, a scout, rushed to Titov's aid. He knocked the dirk out of the officer's hand and stabbed him to death. Then Kozhevnikov shook Titov, convincing himself that he was alive. Afterwards, Kozhevnikov ran ahead to catch up with his comrades, who were pursuing the Nazis that had been rolled back.

When Samusev noticed that two Germans were running away, he rushed at them. His pistol proved empty, so he bent over to snatch a submachine gun from the hands of a wounded German soldier. However, the latter managed to let out a short burst at Samusev's legs. The two Germans whom Samusev had pursued turned around, ran back, and grabbed him under his armpits. In turn, Kozhevnikov rushed at the two Nazis as they were dragging away the Lieutenant toward their trenches. When they saw their pursuer, the Germans let go of Samusev; now they had other things on their minds. Holding the dirk, Kozhevnikov caught up with the Germans and managed to stab one of them to death. He rushed at the second man, and they pitched into each other; they both failed to get up from the ground.

Our troops, including those in our company's sector, were successful in repelling the storm. The Germans left many of their dead and wounded behind on the battlefield; they appeared to have no stomach left for another attack for the time being.

It was December and the twilight deepened quickly. Having dropped their load on Sevastopol and in a hurry to reach their airfields before the onset of darkness, enemy bombers passed overhead, howling. It was quiet in our trenches. The survivors squatted down, greedily sucking on their hand-rolled cigarettes. Nobody was in a mood to talk, for it had been a very trying day. Maksimych stood beside the embrasure, gloomily observing the battlefield.

A new recruit, having apparently decided that his foxhole was too shallow, began to dig, striking his shovel against the limestone. Before anyone could stop him, the Nazis, alerted by the ringing sound, opened up with their mortars. It was already quite dark, but on the right flank Zaytsev's machine gun still pounded away from time to time. The Nazis absolutely refused to quiet down there.

I was still bandaging the wounded when Maksimych came up to me saying that he was going to inspect the left flank, where two blue-eyed young lads manned a light machine gun. He felt that it was too quiet there. When Maksimych made his way to the lads' foxhole, he saw a great many enemy corpses in front of our trenches. Here, too, beside the machine gun wrecked by an explosion, lay both lads. Having dragged the bodies of the machine gunners and their machine gun into the trench, Maksimych covered the corpses with a blood-stained greatcoat. After convincing himself that there were no Germans nearby, the old soldier went to inspect other trenches.

Around this time Ivanova happened to be bandaging the wounded in front of our positions. She heard a single shot, assuming it could only have been fired by an enemy sniper. She got up and looked around to find out who did the sniper fire at. Then she saw Maksimych a few metres away from her. He appeared to have come up against a wall, made a start, dropped his submachine gun, took a single step along the parapet, and then fell.

Ivanova dashed toward the old soldier, dragged him into the trench, and examined his wound.

"I am sorry I haven't accomplished much."

"Don't talk like this, Maksimych!"

"But, I know...."

Ivanova continued bandaging Maksimych's wound, even though she knew it was mortal. He died before she was finished. Though Ivanova had seen a great deal of blood spilled at the front and had witnessed many deaths, she was nevertheless shaken up. To her, as indeed to all of us, Maksimych had been like a father. Yet this was not the time to surrender to grief, so Ivanova left Maksimych's body in the trench and crawled away into the darkness, to render first aid to other wounded soldiers. She had already taken note where they lay, and now confidently crawled along the black battlefield toward them. Since Samusev and Kozhevnikov lay farthest from our positions, she decided to crawl first in that direction. After rolling the unconscious Lieutenant onto a raincape, Ivanova began to crawl back, dragging him toward our trenches; however, when she heard Kozhevnikov moan, she decided to bring them both. Kozhevnikov lay on his back with his arms spread wide apart. His right hand still clutched the dirk of the Nazi officer.

"Who is this, Masha?" Samusev asked quietly; apparently, he came to as a result of the pain he had felt when he was being transferred to the raincape.

"Kozhevnikov," replied Ivanova.

"Is he alive?"

"Yes!"

"Well then, take him first, but leave me a weapon, just in case."

"I can't leave you behind, Lieutenant."

Rolling forcefully off the raincape, Samusev let out a moan.

"What are you trying to do?" exclaimed Ivanova.

"I don't want you to take me first. Kozhevnikov's wounds are more serious."

Samusev pronounced the last few words in a barely audible whisper. The effort cost him dearly, and again he blacked out. Ivanova didn't know what to do. She couldn't take them both at the same time, and she couldn't obey the Lieutenant's order to leave him behind, either; especially after he lost consciousness the second time and in the proximity of enemy positions to boot.

Ivanova pulled the dirk out of Kozhevnikov's hand with difficulty, and began to dress his wounds: shoulder, hip, and head. Despite her gentle touch, she caused him sufficient pain to wake him up. After dressing his wounds, Ivanova pulled him for a short distance toward our trenches. Then she crawled up to Samusev and dragged him for a short distance, too. In this manner, she made her way to our trenches bringing both men.

It was already after midnight when a medical orderly told her that the wounded, including the company commander, were safely delivered to the regimental hospital located in the Inkerman Caves. Both she and I waited impatiently for this news.

As I was helping Ivanova to prepare for the difficult task awaiting her the following day, she pulled out from her boot top a narrow packet wrapped in gauze and quickly opened it up. "Isn't it a great dirk, Zoya?" she said. "I took it away from Kozhevnikov."

"Sister, show it to me!" begged Titov, who was lying nearby.

"Well, if it isn't the very same dirk!" he said excitedly, examining it. "I recognized the dirk by the blue stone in the hilt; it flashed before my eyes while I grappled with the Nazi. He almost stabbed me to death then. Fortunately, one man reached us in time, and saved me from a certain death. I now know his name; it was Kozhevnikov. I am grateful to you, my friend, and I fully intend to repay my debt!"

Following the arrival of the New Year, the Germans conducted themselves quietly, more or less. On both sides active were mainly snipers and combat engineers.

At the beginning of January we gathered in the roomy dugout of the scouts, who were away on a mission. Amongst us were company political instructors, Komsomol organizers and agitators from the entire regiment. Regimental Commissar [political deputy commander] Grigoriy Ivanovich Tsapenko gave a passionate speech about the glorious traditions that had accumulated in our division named after the legendary "Chapay." Each of his words touched one's heart and soul. He received a prolonged applause.

In reaction to the speech, Samarskiy, who was standing beside me, said quietly to scout Nikolay Sizov: "The Commissar is a good lad; I believe I've read all the books there are about Chapayev, but the Commissar talked about things I didn't know. I remember most of it and I'll have a lot to tell to my soldiers."

"I agree with you about the Commissar's speech," replied Sizov. "Only I am not sure that I would be able to retell it to others, even though I, too, remember most of it. But remembering the speech is not enough; one has to have his charisma. And not everyone is so endowed."

After this meeting, modest operational bulletins reflecting individual resources and talent, and with the obligatory portrait of Chapayev, appeared in our dugouts, log emplacements, and permanent strong points. There were artists among the soldiers, and the sections lacking such talent cut out Chapayev's photographs from newspapers and magazines.

One of the soldiers wrote the new "Chapayev lyrics," to the tune of the then very popular song entitled "The Sea Has Spread Over a Wide Area." I must say that the lyrics were far from faultless, but they faithfully expressed the sentiments of our troops. Here is an approximate version:

> The sea has spread over a wide area
> At our dear Crimean shores.
> Like a falcon, Sevastopol stood,
> Ready to battle its enemies.
>
> Seamen, infantrymen and airmen
> Defended the dear city resolutely.
> By the mighty wall of steel
> The bandit met his destiny.
>
> We fought undaunted by heat and cold.
> We grew accustomed to rain and wind.
> Chapayev's children don't falter.
> We'll gain victory in the end.
>
> Go boldly, friends, into the final battle.
> The Motherland will not forget us,
> Ordinary Soviet people.
> We'll stay yours forever, Chapayev.

And then, late one evening, all deserving soldiers and officers were singled out by being given the opportunity to leave the battle zone temporarily, in order to view the film *Chapayev*, which had been miraculously preserved in the besieged city. The film was to be shown in the underground hospital in the Inkerman Caves.

The day before the event had turned out to be very difficult. Many of those who were entitled to see the film fell in the fighting. When finally the battle zone quieted down, as usually happened in the evening, the chosen soldiers, including myself, made themselves presentable with the help of their comrades. (Seeing a movie was an unusual event for us so, naturally, we all tried hard to look our very best.) We left after receiving a warm send-off.

We were given an opportunity to socialize before the film was shown. Recognizing one another, the veterans of Sevastopol's defence quipped that this was the first time they've arrived in the hospital under their own steam, and did not need any medical treatment.

The atmosphere during the viewing of the film was solemn and everyone was touched. As the projector began to chirr and the familiar credit titles appeared on the screen made up of bed sheets, you could sense the soldiers' intense hatred toward the enemy, who had disrupted the lives of all of them. There was so much that struck a responsive chord in us in the first few minutes of the film! The audience consisting of armed soldiers became direct participants, as it were, in the action on the screen. After all, only a few hours earlier they too had rushed at enemy troops, in order to throw them back and crush them.

I saw how the stern men tightened the grip on their weapons, looking as if they were taking aim. The hum of voices spread along the rows. Tension mounted maximally as the enemy marched, to the rolls of the drums, toward the menacingly silent positions of Chapayev troops. Undoubtedly, there was not a single soldier in the room who didn't live through a similar experience. Perhaps the "psychological attacks" of the Germans didn't look as pompous as the one in the film did, but the Nazis were hardly averse to scaring the Russian soldier by their "Prussian contempt for death." Only when it came to the crunch, it turned out that often the Nazis owed their laudible self-control to the consumption of alcohol and other narcotics.

The final frames flashed. A light splash on the water and an enemy bullet kills "Chapay." The Red Cavalry races on. Help comes; and the enemy Whites have good reason to fear for their lives!

We returned to the battle zone in high spirits. That evening each and everyone of us had realized, over and over again, what it meant to be a Chapayev soldier!

When I came back from the Inkerman Caves, I immediately set off for the scouts' dugout, to await their return, as I was instructed to do. The scouts had gone on a mission the previous evening. The group was led by Vasiliy Kozhevnikov, who had recently been released from the hospital.

I didn't have to wait long. A noise came from the trenches, and the first to burst into the dugout was a leggy Nazi officer with hands tied and a woman's kerchief wound around his head. Fearfully looking around, he stopped beside the entrance. Then the scouts brought in a wounded man on a raincape. I recognized him immediately; it was sniper Volodya Zarya, who had not been a member of the scouts' party.

"What has happened?" I asked. "One thing at a time, sister. Let's attend to business first," said Kozhevnikov in a deep voice. Again he looked like a strapping fellow, having completely recovered from his serious wounds. Only after I had bandaged the sniper, Kozhevnikov added: "Sizov and I found him on our way back, as he lay embracing a dead Nazi."

Usually, Zarya went hunting just as it began to get dark. He made his way to the no-man's land by leopard crawl, and set himself up in an ambush prepared beforehand. The no-man's land where Zarya operated was a bare place with split tree stumps, remnants of bushes mowed down by artillery and machine-gun fire, piles of stones, and a multitude of craters of various dimensions, sprinkled over with fresh snow.

On the day he suffered the misfortune, Zarya covered a major portion of the route without a mishap. He had only to crawl a few metres, literally, to the pile of snow-covered stones beside the three thin, split little stumps where his secret hiding place was located. It is common knowledge that illumination quickly changes in the twilight, and the outlines of objects grow less distinct, losing their usual shape. Yet it seemed to Zarya that the slope of the pile of stones behind which he had been accustomed to hide in the past had become more pronounced. He took a better look; everything seemed as usual, but something barely stirred behind the pile of stones. "I must be dreaming," thought Zarya and kept crawling. "Here is the place: a pile of stones with a neat foxhole in a shallow shell crater behind it." He stopped in order to catch his breath before the final spurt. And in that very moment a Nazi with a knife rushed out of Zarya's hideout.

Zarya jumped to his feet, raised his sniper's rifle, and pulled the trigger. No shot followed, so he caught his rifle by the butt and swung it, but the German anticipated his actions and tripped him. Falling, Zarya hit his head against a stone. He felt dizzy but didn't lose consciousness, maybe because he very clearly saw the German's knife suspended over him. But the latter failed to strike Zarya again; anticipating him, the sniper smashed the German's skull with a handy stone.

That very same night, we sent Zarya to a medical battalion. The next morning the scouts barely had enough time for all the visitors that came to see them, for it was a quiet day. The door kept opening, and acquaintances from other sections and companies kept dropping into the dugout, to inquire after the successful mission and to hear all the details of Zarya's story, or simply to pass the time with comrades. Anatoliy Samarskiy with his inseparable accordion came as well. They said that singing followed Samarskiy no matter where he went. The men barely began to sing "The Dugout" [a popular wartime love song—Trans.], when Commissar Tsapenko appeared. The duty man jumped up, but the Commissar made a sign that they should continue singing.

Then they were interrupted by the postman. "Jump for joy, guys!" he exclaimed while still on the threshold. We expected him to come the previous day. He placed his heavy bag on the table and, like a conjurer, kept producing one envelope after another. "Rejoice, guys! Ships have come from the Mainland! There are letters for everybody in the battalion," the postman shouted. "And not only letters," he added, winking at us conspiratorially.

After distributing the mail, the postman approached the Commissar and whispered confidentially: "Parcels have arrived, too, and are being sorted in the regimental dugout by the soldiers of the HQ defence platoon. Just in time for the Red Army's anniversary."

With the onset of darkness, delegations from various battalions kept arriving in the dugout, to claim the gifts from the Mainland. Kozhevnikov, the smart and tall commander of the scouts who was to become the hero of the day, had joined our group. I daresay it was only then that I noticed that he had regular features and large, grey eyes.

"Here, Comrade Senior Sergeant, take this gift intended for you personally," said the Commissar handing Kozhevnikov one of the parcels. "And you needn't look so surprised. I am not mistaken. You are now Senior Sergeant; you've been promoted out of turn."

"I serve the Soviet Union!" was Kozhevnikov's regulation response.

"Do provide a good example to your subordinates, always and everywhere," said the Commissar.

Kozhevnikov lost his composure. The events of the past twenty-four hours proved too much for him. Unnerved, he departed somewhat from the regulation response: "I'll do my best, Comrade Commissar."

When he returned to his dugout, Kozhevnikov carefully opened the parcel and laid out its contents on the table: a piece of toilet soap, an embroidered tobacco pouch, a fountain pen, a pair of warm socks, a bottle of eau-de-cologne, and two chocolade bars.

"What's the point of all this," Kozhevnikov drawled out, and with a guilty look on his face began to crush in his hands the little linen bag which had held the presents. "Brothers, let's share it," he said earnestly.

"Eh, no!" responded Nikolay Sizov. "Commissar's orders. The gift parcel is strictly for you. After all, we haven't been forgotten, either; each of us has received something. But look here, Comrade Senior Sergeant" —Sizov underlined the new rank of Kozhevnikov—"you've not taken everything out of the parcel."

"What do you mean?" asked Kozhevnikov.

"Allow me." However, Kozhevnikov forestalled Sizov and himself examined the little bag. "You're right! It's a letter!"

"Of course. There has to be a letter!" Sizov looked over Kozhevnikov's shoulder and read the address: "To the bravest defender of Sevastopol."

"So that's why he got this parcel," exclaimed Sizov. "He deserves it!"

"He deserves it, indeed," agreed the scouts.

Kozhevnikov ripped the envelope open and read out: "My dear soldier and defender of Sevastopol! All the best to you and your comrades on the occasion of the 24th anniversary of the Red Army. I wish you good health, happiness, and new successes in combat. Here is a modest gift for you. Should you have a spare moment, please write me about your exploits at the front."

After he finished reading the letter, Kozhevnikov grew pensive and sad. "Comrade Senior Sergeant!" Sizov addressed him formally. He knew why his commander and fellow countryman was upset. Their home region had been occupied by the Germans, who did as they liked there. "Now you've someone to exchange correspondence with. And the fine girl sent you a fountain pen, envelopes and writing paper."

It was quiet in the scouts' dugout. The soldiers sat at the table, enjoying their flagrant gift cigarettes. Silently, without consulting one another, they made room for their commander so that he could write a reply. Kozhevnikov sat down and bent over a piece of paper.

"And what should I write concerning Sevastopol?" he asked as he was finishing the letter.

"Do write that we'll stand to the last man," said Sizov on behalf of everyone present.

Then and there the curious Sizov tried to take a peek at the letter over Kozhevnikov's shoulder, but the latter gently pushed him away. So nobody ever learned what Kozhevnikov had written to the girl whose gift parcel was addressed "To the bravest defender of Sevastopol." However, everybody knew that Kozhevnikov did not hand the letter to the postman, but dropped it the next day directly into the field mail box in the Inkerman Caves, after he and Sizov arrived there to visit Zarya in the underground hospital.

The huge interior of the Inkerman Caves was divided into "wards" with bed sheets. As Kozhevnikov and Sizov were entering one such ward, they ran into military surgeon Mariya Andreyevna Antonova. She frowned when she saw them, but did not scold them for not wearing the regulation white smocks. They stopped expectantly, holding out their packages and bags with gifts for Zarya.

"Are you the lads who saved the sniper?" asked Antonova.

"Indeed we are," nodded Sizov. "He is my superior and I am his subordinate. We are on our way to visit the sniper, Volodya Zarya."

"I am not going to let you see him until this evening and on the condition that the wounded man has improved," said Antonova. She didn't want to disturb Zarya who had been delirious and had just fallen asleep after a restless night.

"Is his condition serious?" asked Sizov.

"Zarya lost a great deal of blood, but I daresay he'll recover by May Day and might well increase his score by that time."

"Thank you, doctor," uttered Sizov, attempting to mollify her, and intentionally let out a loud sigh.

"Cut this out!" said Antonova sternly. She saw through Sizov's strategy to gain her sympathy. "I've already made an exception for you. Otherwise, I might just not let you see him in the evening, either."

"We are so..." began Sizov.

"By the look of your commander I can tell that you have been given leave only until this evening," said Antonova and smiled. "In the meantime, go to the Reading Room, where you can pass the time reading newspapers and magazines. When it becomes possible for you to see your comrade, I'll call you."

Antonova accompanied them to the passage leading to the Reading Room, and then she went away. When she was out of sight, Sizov turned to Kozhevnikov, and said: "Comrade Senior Sergent, you are so eloquent when you keep quiet that women see right through you."

"Eh, Sizov, Sizov.... The rattle of machine-gun fire doesn't bother me, but after spending a while with you I develop a splitting headache."

"I believe it is useful."

"A headache?"

"Of course, not! I mean my talking to people. But a headache can best be cured with a good cigarette in the fresh air. All the same, my talking is useful! If I hadn't told the duty nurse what hero you're, Senior Sergeant, they wouldn't have let us into the hospital."

"Oh, Nikolay... don't be so formal, my fellow countryman."

They stopped at the exit from the Caves and began to smoke.

The sound of children's laughter nearby was so unexpected that they were both startled. A flock of boys and girls wearing Young Pioneer [junior branch of the Komsomol—Trans.] neckties ran out from behind a corner, and began to play "hide and seek." When a snub-nosed little fellow hid behind Sizov to evade his pursuers, the latter involuntarily exclaimed: "I bet you help in looking after the wounded in the hospital, yet you make noise like little children; it's not nice."

"We do go to school here! Our school is also located in the Caves. We are on our break. And who are you?"

"We came from the battle zone," said Sizov pompously.

"Then how come you don't even know that we're going to school here? And we sent you so many gifts! Perhaps you haven't received them yet?" The children stopped playing and surrounded the soldiers.

"The front is vast. Gifts were sent to other divisions as well," remarked Sizov reasonably.

"We've sent our gifts to the Chapayev Division itself! And that's the truth!"

"Children, the Division is big...."

"So who received our gifts?"

"Obviously, the bravest soldiers did," said Kozhevnikov.

"And do you know them?"

"We do," confirmed Sizov authoritatively. "Since you sent your gifts to the Chapayev Division, only heroes would have received them. Everyone in our division is a hero."

"We were in the hospital yesterday. We go there every day, to read newspapers and books to the wounded...." a little girl with pigtails said resolutely. She suddenly stopped short and, somewhat bewildered, began to blink her eyes. "Do you know anything about the sniper who was brought in here yesterday? He fought hand-to-hand with a German that stabbed our man, who afterwards killed the German with a stone."

"Some scouts saved this sniper," a shock-headed boy joined in the conversation. "And on top of that, they captured a Nazi. Eh, if only one could meet these men!"

Sizov felt a shove from behind, administered to him by Kozhevnikov to make him keep quiet.

The bell rang, so the schoolchildren ran into the Caves. For a long time, Kozhevnikov kept following them with his eyes and then said quietly: "It is they, after all, who are the true heroes."

Sizov nodded in agreement, even though he had the reputation of an inveterate arguer, who reacted to every life's situation with an outlook or opinion of his own, sometimes highly peculiar.

When the two friends entered the Reading Room, they greedily pounced on some magazines, as they hadn't read any for several months. Afterwards they played a game of checkers, and later on also one of dominoes with some patients on the mend. It was here that they were found by the military surgeon Antonova. "You may go in now. For exactly two minutes," she said.

The visit turned out to be even shorter. While Sizov attempted to stuff Zarya's presents into his nightstand, which was already quite full, Kozhevnikov greeted Zarya on behalf of his comrades, the regimental commanding officer Zakharov and Commissar Tsapenko. However, the sniper was still very weak. When he saw his rescuers, he got excited and grew very pale, so Doctor Antonova at once sent the visitors packing.

Meanwhile, the scouts anxiously awaited a reply to their commander's letter. As soon as the postman appeared in the dugout, the first thing a soldier would do was to ask him in a whisper whether the reply to Kozhevnikov's letter had arrived. However, there was no mail for Kozhevnikov. Finally, exactly three weeks after Kozhevnikov had mailed his letter, the postman burst into the dugout with a solemn and mysterious look: "You've a letter, Comrade Senior Sergeant! A thick one! With a photograph inside, no doubt!"

Indeed, there was a snapshot in the envelope. Sizov reached for the photograph and took it out of Kozhevnikov's hand. "What a beauty! You're a lucky man, Comrade Senior Sergeant!" Everyone agreed with Sizov: "She is a beauty, without a doubt!" The dugout quickly emptied to let the Senior Sergeant read the letter in peace and compose a reply. The last to leave were Sizov and the postman; the latter informed Sizov confidentially that the Commissar himself was interested in Kozhevnikov's letter.

"Nonsense!" muttered Sizov and made it clear that he did not wish to pursue the matter. It was only much later that I learned how well the joker Sizov could keep a secret. After the gifts had been delivered to the Regiment, Commissar Tsapenko and Sizov purposely selected a parcel for Kozhevnikov with a letter in it. As to Kozhevnikov's correspondence with the donor: well, that was another matter.

The short and pleasant Crimean spring had arrived. It was an odd sight to behold how light green blades of grass suddenly shot up from the mutilated ground, saturated with powder fumes and smelling of explosives. A few days later, white and blue snowdrops broke out through the grass. Cut by shrapnel, trees and bushes became covered with delicate green leaves.

The battle zone came to life, too. Our soldiers hollowed out the rock with a point-tool, digging in deeper and deeper. They covered themselves —including the head—with two greatcoats, to prevent the enemy from hearing the blows, since the Germans immediately reacted to any and every movement in our trenches, opening up with mortars.

All the infantrymen had bloody blisters on their hands and battered fingers, but each of them continued to nibble at the folds of the Mekenziyevyye Mountains. They toiled around the clock in shifts. Our permanent strong points and log emplacements were built at night, and then the structures were thoroughly camouflaged. Of course, everybody trained in handling Soviet-made weapons every day and was also becoming accustomed to the captured ones, since the scouts brought in a lot of them.

The Nazis didn't loaf either, and kept reinforcing their positions. Meanwhile, the scouts went on reconnaissance missions, fixed the locations of enemy engineer works, and transmitted the data to our artillery men. In turn, by night the latter pounded to bits all that the Nazis accomplished by day. The Nazis also keenly followed our activities. Their twin-fuselage spy plane hovered over us for hours, and their artillery and mortar bombardments became a daily occurrence. The enemy concentrated his forces for a new attack.

One sunny day, we spread out several raincapes on the ground in the vicinity of the regimental HQ; then we brought in a Maxim machine gun and began to study it. The gathering included regimental scouts, snipers, signallers, and soldiers of the HQ defence platoon. It was a routine lesson, and the soldiers replied smartly to the instructor's questions.

Unexpectedly, Nina Onilova appeared amongst us. The heroine of the defence of Odessa, particularly of the December battles, she was a machine gunner well-known to all at Sevastopol. Nina had been dropping in on us quite often. We became good friends and I frequently complained to her that, even though I had been allowed to come back to the front from the hospital, I was currently employed mainly as a medic, on the pretext that there were no vacancies in our machine-gun companies. Nina kept reassuring me in a friendly manner. I knew that she had already intervened with my superiors on several occasions, but so far to no avail.

Our men greeted Onilova with joy. "Nina, tell us your secret," asked Kozhevnikov.

"What secret are you talking about?" replied Onilova with a smile.

"How do you manage to kill one hundred Germans with one hundred rounds?"

"Fancy that! If it were true, I would soon be left with nothing to do. And those who don't work, don't eat!"

"Don't worry," someone reassured her. "We've only two women machine gunners amongst us. You and our Medvedeva. We'll manage to provide for you both somehow."

"Well, that's great...." said Nina and went down beside the machine gun. She stripped and assembled the Maxim so quickly that the soldiers were awestruck.

"What class..." several men said in unison.

"The main thing, guys, is to remember about the breech-block, the heart of the machine gun."

Onilova was so quick in stripping and assembling the breech-block that it took our breath away. Then she told us how she selected reference points for aimed fire both by day and night. She expressed an interest in the whereabouts of the machine gun's extra breech-block and its spare parts. We were made ashamed of the Maxim's operator, who was commander of the HQ defence platoon's machine-gun crew. "I don't have one.... And I can't get one," he confessed, throwing up his hands.

"You don't say so!" Onilova exclaimed with indignation. "Imagine, you are in a battle and firing your machine gun. Suddenly, something breaks down. There is no time to strip the breech-block and replace the broken part. The enemy is pressing hard. What are you going to do? You are alive; there is a lot of ammunition left and plenty of water in the machine gun's cooling jacket, but the machine gun has been silenced. And the Nazis are killing your comrades! Who is at fault? You are! You are a poor machine gunner and a poor comrade!"

Bewildered, the operator of the Maxim didn't reply.

"This is a serious matter," concluded Onilova.

"Never mind," said one of the soldiers sitting nearby. "We'll get another breech-block and all of its little parts before your next visit."

"You mustn't forget, guys. I'll come the day after tomorrow to check," warned Nina.

"We'll get one without fail," I confirmed.

"Well, well, Zoya, we shall see."

"Tell me frankly, where do you get spare parts for your Maxim?" I asked.

"All right, I'll tell you," said Onilova with a smile. "Have you heard of the armourers in the Inkerman Caves? If they haven't got a breech-block, don't be lazy and get one from the factory."

"What kind of factory is this?" I asked her.

"The former 'Hammer' Repair Workshops in Sevastopol, which used to fix Primus stoves as well as pots and pans. It functions as a munitions plant now. The master craftsmen who work there each have a wonderful pair of hands. They can make anything you need. I'll get a spare breech-block for you, Zoya, myself. Only transfer to machine-gun duty as soon as you can."

All that remained for me to do was to let out a sigh. After all, no one was better aware of my cherished dream than Nina!

"What's going on here?" exclaimed Colonel Nikolay Zakharov, the commanding officer of our regiment, while approaching us. "And I thought that Onilova was teaching my machine gunners useful things, but apparently I was mistaken. I am disappointed!"

"She has already finished the lesson, Comrade Colonel," replied Kozhevnikov.

"What did she teach you, for example?"

Kozhevnikov reported on the lesson, including our embarrassment due to the missing spare breech-block.

Zakharov acquired a stern look: "We'll deal with the problem later.... Do the soldiers know the machine gun well?"

"Too bad I have not been provided with a logbook," replied Onilova. "Otherwise, I would have rated everyone 'excellent'!"

"And her, too?" Zakharov nodded in my direction.

"I've not examined Zoya. I'll do it next time, Comrade Colonel."

"No, do it now! Knowing Zoya's preoccupation with machine guns, I want you to examine her now, in my presence. Then we'll decide where she belongs."

"Do I have your permission to begin?" I asked.

"Go ahead."

I answered all of the Onilova's questions. At Colonel Zakharov's request I listed all the possible causes of jamming that may occur during firing, and ways of remedying them. Of course, I was very nervous. While replying I kept looking at Nina to determine whether my answers were correct. The expression on her face told me that I was doing fine.

"Very good," said Zakharov, smiling cunningly. "Now here is the final question: 'What was the location of the stock plates on the Chapayev machine gun?'" I lowered my eyes. It was not difficult for me to guess what Zakharov had in mind; the heavy machine gun doesn't have stock plates; it has slides in the side plates of breech casing. They were called "stock plates" by Pet'ka in the film *Chapayev*, while Pet'ka was instructing Anka, Chapayev's famous woman soldier, in the handling of machine guns. I figured it all out immediately, but was too shy to say it aloud.

"There is no such question in the Manual, Comrade Colonel. I can't answer it."

"Well, that settles it," said Colonel Zakharov. He didn't sound annoyed. "You'll carry a medical bag for the time being. But I respect you as a woman of principle. Well, all right. As for you, Nina, can you strip the machine gun, blindfolded?" he asked.

"At home, in my log emplacement, I manage to do it in only 30 to 40 seconds."

"You are our guest, and I'll give you a minute."

Onilova's performance was brilliant. Then Zakharov proposed that Kozhevnikov announce a break. The men and officers sat down on spread out raincapes, made themselves comfortable, and smoked with pleasure. Nina lit up too, so I gave her a look of disapproval.

"Don't be angry at me, friend." She gave me the wink. "When the Allies open the Second Front, I'll quit immediately. I mean it."

"Suppose we smash the Nazis before the Second Front is opened? What then?" asked Zakharov.

"I'll then smoke two cigarettes, one after another. One, out of joy, to celebrate the victory, the other, out of sadness, to mourn the many comrades who didn't live to see the happy day."

From the battle zone came the sound of long bursts fired with our machine guns. Zakharov hurriedly set off for his dugout, to be near the telephone. Nina got up and was ready to leave too. I accompanied her part of the way and we hugged each other at parting.

"I'll come the day after tomorrow!" she shouted, already from a distance. I followed her with my eyes for a long time. Like all defenders of Sevastopol, I was very fond of Nina, a simple and merry young girl, yet a bold and brave soldier. As in the past, I still dreamed of transferring to Onilova's unit and becoming No. 2 of her machine-gun crew.

I found Colonel Zakharov in the dugout of the HQ defence platoon that was filled with soldiers standing at attention. Since there was no room for me inside, I stood at the entrance. Beside the table, I saw the No. 1 of the platoon's machine-gun crew (the one who was missing a spare breech-block) nervously shifting his feet. I slowly raised myself on my tiptoes and noticed a breech-block, together with its rusted spare parts, lying on a dirty rag spread out on the table.

"I knew you had them."

"I am so ashamed, Comrade Colonel," answered the soldier, red as a lobster. "I put them away, back in the fall, and forgot all about them."

What an explanation! Oh, I got so mad at the blunderer! He was degraded and sent to a rifle company. In my opinion, the punishment was well deserved.

Nina Onilova kept her word. She arrived at the appointed time and immediately asked: "Have you obtained the spare parts for the machine gun?"

"Here, Comrade Inspector, is the breech-block and accessories," reported the new commander of the HQ defence platoon's machine-gun crew.

"Well done! And this is for you, Zoya. A present from me." She handed me a breech-block and accessories, which she had promised to bring. "You're now almost a machine gunner!" Then she took out a few violets from her breast pocket and said: "This is for good luck. And here are the other things I promised to bring—a notebook and an exercise-book."

"What for?" asked the men, curious.

"Let her write down everything she observes," replied Nina. "I, too, am keeping a diary. And when we have gained victory, Zoya and I will publicize the exploits of each and every one of you. By the way, Zoya, let's call on the commander of your regiment. Perhaps he'll turn out to be in a better mood today."

On the way, I couldn't resist opening the notebook. Here is what Nina had carefully printed on the first page:

"Fighting comes easily to you, if you don't think about dying. You must understand, without fail, the cause in which you are risking your young life. If you seek glory for its own sake—that's bad. Only those exploits are commendable that are inspired by love for one's people and country. Always keep in mind that you are defending your country; and heroism and glory will then come to you of their own accord." [This version differs slightly from the one cited in the Appendix—Trans.]

Zakharov received us with a smile. "Well, to forestall your calling on me every other day, I better let Medvedeva join a machine-gun company immediately. This will be my gift to her on the occasion of International Women's Day, 8 March, which is rapidly approaching, so you, Nina, must join us without fail in celebrating the holiday. We'll treat you to cherry jam and tea, served in a genuine cup and saucer, rather than an aluminum mug."

"All right, Comrade Colonel!" replied Nina merrily. "After all, I must give Zoya a send-off."

It was quiet in the battle zone on 8 March, but a sudden telephone ring broke the silence in the regimental dugout. The duty officer took the receiver off the hook. After an exchange of the passwords, a voice at the other end of the line said: "Yesterday evening Nina was badly wounded [inaccurate; Onilova had been wounded a week earlier—Trans.]; and she died in the hospital."

"Who are you talking about?" the duty officer asked.

"Onilova, as I've just told you, was wounded yesterday. She died...."

"Nina! We are expecting her. We've prepared gifts for her."

"So did we. Only there was no time to present them to her."

I was there, in the dugout. I heard what was being said about Nina and I didn't believe it. I cried and I didn't believe it. But it was true.

On that very same day, I handed over my medical bag to a nurse who had just returned from a hospital, and set off for the battle zone to join the machine-gun platoon commanded by Junior Lieutenant Pavel Andreyevich Morozov, a veteran of the Civil War. Already over forty, Morozov nevertheless seemed to be a great deal younger due to his exceptionally smart appearance. A thickset man, he had a round kind face on which large grey eyes shone. Morozov disliked having greying hair and constantly shaved his head to get rid of it.

When I introduced myself to him, Morozov looked me over attentively. Aware of his high standards, I made sure that I looked my best.

"Well, little daughter, it seems that you've come here for good."

"For good, indeed."

Then the Commissar, who happened to be paying a visit to the platoon to attend to some matters, assured Morozov that if he can't take me, a place would be found for me in another platoon. Morozov looked very seriously at Tsapenko and replied with confidence: "She'll stay. To tell the truth, Comrade Commissar, we came to an agreement about this a long time ago. Back then I promised Medvedeva that I'll make her the No. 1 of a machine-gun crew. And should there be no vacancies, well then, I'll step down to No. 2 myself. "Welcome to the platoon, Medvedeva." Then he added in a fatherly fashion: "Don't worry, you'll be well treated."

So this was how I've realized my dream.

During relative calm, the soldiers of Morozov's platoon did not twiddle their thumbs. The commander himself expertly handled all types of regimental weapons and expected the same of his subordinates. Each of his men could handle company mortars and anti-tank guns too, if necessary, in the capacity of any crew number.

I mastered various types of weapons under the supervision of Sergeant Andrey Zaytsev, my acquaintance of long standing, who happened to be Morozov's deputy. He no longer looked the absent-minded lad I remember running into on my way to the front, but had become a knowledgeable and very strict commander.

Around this time spring weather was asserting itself more and more. It was a hotter sun that warmed up the mutilated earth. The air became filled with the smell of new greenery, which grew swiftly after the abundant spring showers.

A twin-fuselage spy plane hung over our heads for days at a time. Enemy bombers flew toward Sevastopol in ever greater numbers. Anti-aircraft guns fired at them with intensified ferocity, spreading cloudlets of explosions over the blue sky.

The commander ordered us to improve the camouflage of our dugouts, permanent strong points, log emplacements, and some trenches. They were covered tightly with thin tree trunks, and turf was placed on this roof. Even approaches, such as narrow paths, were camouflaged, so that they would not be seen from above by a Nazi air observer. And to one side appeared slogans, composed of small stones: "Death to German invaders! We would rather die than give ground!"

Even though the weather was spoiling us, it was capricious in spring-like fashion. One day, the sky became overcast in the early evening. A strong wind blew in a storm. Large, warm rain drops fell to the ground. Morozov was resting in our dugout. He woke up, having apparently mistaken a clap of thunder for an artillery strike. He got up quickly, took a raincape, and went out to inspect the sentry posts. He came back in about two hours soaked right through; he had given his raincape to a sentry. The expression on his face indicated that everything was in order.

The off-duty soldiers in the permanent strong point were awake. For a long time, I stood beside the embrasure. A gusty wind blew in tiny raindrops. After covering the machine gun with my greatcoat, I sat down near the embrasure. My heart was heavy and I felt troubled. Flashes of lightning, resembling reflections of explosions, burst through the open door into the permanent strong point. After the noise of the thunder had died down, for a long time you could still hear how the little streams of dry, stony soil fell somewhere behind one of the walls.

Morozov was sitting down on the ground at the exit from the pillbox, smoking a hand-rolled cigarette. Almost inaudibly, he hummed a song about a raging storm and the murmur of rain. Anatoliy Samarskiy quietly joined in. Beside the pillbox stood Kurbatov, the sentry (a very young soldier who was the ammunition number). Covered with a raincape, he peered—until his eyes hurt—into the darkness which was becoming more and more impenetrable after each flash of lightning. A narrow lane, cleared in the minefield and intended for our scouts, began where Kurbatov stood. It was a winding trail which disappeared into the ravine.

During one such flash of lightning Kurbatov saw a group of men walking along the path. At first he couldn't believe his eyes, but when lightning flashed again, the young soldier became convinced that a group of men were indeed coming out of the ravine. He was overjoyed, thinking they were friendly troops returning from a mission.

Kurbatov wrapped his raincape around himself tighter. When only a few steps remained between him and the approaching soldiers, he demanded the regulation "Halt!" and "Password?" There was no answer. "Halt!" he repeated and clicked the breech-block of his submachine gun. Before he had a chance to fire he was hit over the head and stunned. Subsequently, several grenades exploded beside the pillbox.

Morozov dashed toward the embrasure. Groping his way in the dark, he hastily placed the barrel of our machine gun opposite the peg "reference point two" and fired a long burst at the trail. Then he fired another burst. He listened for a while and then, with his Nagant revolver at the ready, ran to the spot where the sentry had stood only a few minutes earlier. He called Kurbatov, but there was no answer. The soldiers alerted by Sergeant Zaytsev joined Morozov, panting.

"They kidnapped him...."

"That's right; the vile creatures dragged him away."

"Poor lad."

"Goof! He thought they were friendly...."

Listening to the exclamations of his soldiers, Morozov kept silent. He was obviously upset, for the kidnapping of a sentry was a serious matter. After posting new sentries, he returned to the dugout and rolled himself a new, thick cigarette.

In our platoon no one cared to sleep that night and everyone was in a rotten mood. Meanwhile, the storm calmed down and a thick impenetrable mist went up in the early morning. Then Morozov was summoned to the HQ and spent a long time there. He came back, refused to eat, and chain-smoked fat hand-rolled cigarettes.

The night was quiet. The trees slept, as it were, tired out by bad weather. After a sunny day, the wormwood smelled overpoweringly. I was to do guard duty from 10.00 p.m. until midnight beside the small path cleared of mines, so Zaytsev kept briefing me for about an hour. All the same, he wouldn't let me do guard duty alone and stood nearby himself, in addition to Morozov (who admitted later on that he was waiting for the return of the German scouts).

Around midnight I noted that "reference point two"—the wild-rose bush at the turn of the narrow path—appeared to move, so I alerted the commander. He, Zaytsev, and I waited vigilantly. Then a group of soldiers came out from behind the rose bush.

"Alert the machine gunners!" ordered our commander and then turned to me: "You're to go back to the pillbox and stay there, by the Maxim."

"I am on sentry duty, Comrade Junior Lieutenant."

"It's an order!" he admonished me.

The night was bright, moonlit, and there were many stars. Through the embrasure I clearly distinguished our machine gunners headed by Morozov, beside the path. I also saw the men getting out of the ravine. They already were half way up the slope. The one who was in the lead appeared to have two heads, one above the other.

"Halt! The Password?" I heard Morozov shouting.

"We are friendly."

A few wearisome seconds passed. I looked at the men climbing the slope of ravine through the notch of my sight. "Halt!" repeated Morozov. "Or I'll shoot!"

The one walking in the lead replied, breathing hard: "We're friendly...

scouts... carrying a wounded man."

"They're friendly, Comrade Platoon Commander," confirmed Kurbatov in a weak voice. "They brought me along."

Morozov went down the path carefully: "Indeed they're friendly.... Kurbatov, you're alive!" he exclaimed.

"Yes, Sir!"

"I knew you'll outsmart them in the end," said Morozov.

Several machine gunners went down the path to help carry Kurbatov, who was wounded in both legs, into the trench. After leaving him in the care of a medic, Morozov scolded the scouts' commander: "How come you took so long? You'll get into trouble!"

"It couldn't be helped; the *relatives* moved to a new address, so we wasted a lot of time looking for them. We were so excited that we didn't even notice him," replied one of the scouts, nodding toward a stout German without a head-dress and with hands tied behind his back.

"It seems to me he is a staff officer," said Morozov.

"Quite likely.... The Colonel will be able to tell. On top of that we saved your soldier on the way. This should also count in our favour."

Kurbatov came to when his Nazi captors began to descend into the ravine. He saw that his hands were tightly bound with a string and he was gagged. Then a machine-gun burst fired from our pillbox caught up with two of the Germans who were bringing up the rear. They fell dead, and those in the lead abandoned their prisoner, dashing past the turn in the road where the dead zone began, beyond the reach of our machine gun.

Kurbatov jumped up, flung himself to one side, and with a superhuman effort expelled the gag from his mouth. However, he barely managed to run fifteen paces in the bushes when a new misfortune overtook him; an anti-tank mine which had exploded nearby wounded him in both legs. Fearful that the Germans might return, he lay hidden in the bushes, forcing himself not to moan. Kurbatov knew that by calling for help he would only be drawing enemy attention to himself, as he was too far from friendly troops to be heard by them.

Having lost a great deal of blood, Kurbatov was too weak to attempt crawling toward friendly troops. He managed to free his hands, but the effort exhausted him and he blacked out. When he came to the next morning and saw hillocks all around, he realized that these mounds were German anti-personnel mines covered with earth. He also noticed a deep aerial bomb crater, half-filled with rain water. He had no choice but to lower himself into the hole and lay in this "bathtub" all day long, with only his head sticking above the surface.

At twilight Kurbatov again stole up to the path, having previously marked out the route. Here he was found by the scouts returning home from an area behind enemy lines. This happened just before May Day, and we were happy that our machine-gun platoon was, after all, spared the extra ignominy of losing a sentry so close to the holiday.

The next day, 30 April, on the eve of May Day, a Party meeting was held; the main item on the agenda was admission of new members. That day, among those admitted to the Party was Sergeant Andrey Zaytsev. However, immediately after the distribution of festive gifts, a terrible artillery strike was brought down upon us. Yet the next morning all the soldiers and officers—mindful of the holiday—attached clean inside collars to their field shirts, and polished their shoes and boots with home-made shoe cream until they shone.

Regardless of the difficult situation, we solemnly celebrated the May Day holiday. I daresay the happiest May Day was that of Fedor Tkachenko, the political instructor of our company, for his wife came from the Mainland to join him. From the very beginning of the war, Olya Tkachenko, who was then nursing her infant son, was keen to serve at the front. She waited about a year until the child was older, and then she left him with his grandmother and came to the besieged Sevastopol to serve as a medical NCO.

The appointment did not come easy to her, since the battalion commander was at first highly reluctant to permit Olya Tkachenko to serve alongside her husband. She was told that wives were not allowed in the battle zone. "If only Fedor and I could serve in the same battalion," she insisted.

"All right," said the battalion commander, giving in the end. "I'll discuss the matter with Major Antipin, the new commanding officer of our regiment...." (Mikhail Stepanovich Antipin replaced Colonel Nikolay Vasil'yevich Zakharov, who had been transferred to a naval infantry brigade.) It turned out that Antipin didn't object, so husband and wife Fedor and Olya Tkachenko both served in the battalion to which our company belonged.

One day, Major-General Trofim Kalinovich Kolomiyets, our divisional commander, and Colonel Parfentiy Grigor'yevich Neustroyev, his chief of staff, arrived at our regimental HQ. After greeting warmly Major Antipin and his chief of staff Major Shestopalov, the General straight off began inspecting the recently built dugout smelling of fresh logs. Meanwhile, Major Shestopalov quickly unrolled a map on the table, on which the defensive line of Lieutenant Samusev's company, recently evened out, was traced with thick red pencil. "Don't bother with the map for the time being. First all, I want to make an inspection together with your regimental commanding officer, to determine what your conditions really are," said the General, walking toward the exit.

"Ring up No. 2 battalion," Antipin told Shestopalov in a low voice, taking the map case. "No," objected Shestopalov just as quietly, looking at the half-closed door. "The General doesn't like to have his arrival advertised beforehand. It is a good thing that he paid us a visit first. He usually goes directly to company dispositions. He is very well informed as to the state of our regimental defences. Moreover, he knows many soldiers and officers."

"So we meet again," said the General extending his hand to Morozov. "You haven't changed—shaving your head both in winter and summer. It seems that your grey head of hair is an embarrassment to you and you wish to conceal, from your young people, the fact that you've gone grey—isn't so? And how are you keeping?"

"Fine, thank you. So far, I've nothing to complain about."

"Is the mail delivery regular? Do you often hear from your wife?"

"It depends, Comrade General; sometimes she writes frequently, and sometimes I don't hear from her for a long time."

"So you're here too, Comrade Zaytsev! Why are you hiding behind the back of your commanding officer? Such a good soldier, and yet so afraid of his General!" he quipped.

"I am not afraid of you," retorted Zaytsev, embarrassed.

"Your new permanent strong point is not bad," continued the General. "Yet the approaches to it are useless; the trench is only knee-deep in places. You ought to dig in deeper, deeper into the ground, before it's too late," he added, seriously concerned.

"How? There is nothing here but rock," Morozov objected.

"Well then, bite into the rock."

"Easier said than done," countered Morozov, "for the Nazis reply to every sound we make by laying dozens of mines. Though we would dearly love to do it, we can't extend our defences; the accursed enemy is too close."

The General was silent for a while, and then uttered in a low voice: "I know you're unhappy. Doing nothing bores you—isn't so? Well, question me; don't be shy."

"Why should we be shy; we've known you as far back as the fighting for Odessa," replied Zaytsev on everyone's behalf. "We've only one question: 'When will the fighting start?'"

"All in good time. Have some fun and rest for a while. It won't be long now. It won't be long; not at all!" repeated the General, leaving. Our divisional commander didn't gallop, as Chapayev did, on a spirited horse, and lacked Chapayev's splendid moustache, but all those who had known Chapayev were saying that the General somehow reminded them of him. Simple and warm-hearted, he knew how to approach every soldier—with a kind word, a joke, and a fatherly scolding, if necessary. He earned his men's respect, and what's more, their affection.

After strolling around several dugouts and permanent strong points, the General returned to the HQ. "Boris Anisimovich, now is the time to unroll the map," he told Shestopalov. "Let's take a look at the area defended by No. 1 battalion." The General bent over the map and continued after a pause: "We're not going to straighten out the defensive line, but there is a need to deepen the trenches, if possible, between No. 1 and No. 2 companies, and to make a thick earthy rampart on all dugouts and ceilings of trenches. Also, the first shock wave is bound to knock down the permanent strong point which had been constructed a week ago at the boundary with No. 3 company. You're not looking after your machine gunners properly."

"I've already issued an order to prepare the logs, Comrade General," replied Major Antipin.

"And see to it that your mortar men shoot down into the ravine. I suspect the enemy will gather there for an attack. Well, since the logs have already been ordered, I've nothing more to say." Then he turned to Neustroyev, his chief of staff: "Have you anything to add?"

"Only one item; we need a prisoner for interrogation, and a good one to boot." That same night three scouts led by Senior Sergeant Kozhevnikov set off for the front lines along the narrow lane cleared by our engineers. The path was well guarded; a searchlight placed by the Nazis on a high bluff lit up the undergrowth at the bottom of the ravine every five minutes or so. As soon as the beam went out, one after another flares kept shooting up into the dark sky. The scouts had to keep going to ground, like a stone, every two to three steps. And yet the men managed to steal up very closely to enemy positions. "Comrade Major, your order has been executed," Kozhevnikov reported to Antipin at daybreak. "Unfortunately, the prisoner for interrogation turned out to be unimportant—a mere corporal in the artillery troops. However, we saw something interesting going on among our *neighbours*." And he described new German firing points as well as freshly dug trenches and foxholes, scattered like a spider web in front of the Chapayev Division lines.

The reconnaissance data and the prisoner's testimony confirmed that the enemy was preparing another storm. With each day, the situation at the front was becoming more and more alarming. A meeting of the delegates from our division, as well as the famous attached battalion of naval gunners commanded by Major V.A. Odynets, was held in the second half of May. On the podium, beside senior line officers—Major-General Kolomiyets, Regimental Commissar Rasnikov, as well as Fink, Head of the Divisional Political Section—sat our comrades, representatives of troops in the battle zone.

Here, in a front-line grove, we were told that Soviet troops had abandoned Kerch' and the enemy intensively transferred men and equipment to Sevastopol, concentrating them in the area of Mekenziyevyye Mountains, in front of the lines of our Chapayev Division. Ending his speech, Rasnikov, on behalf of the Independent Maritime Army's Military Council and the command of our division, appealed to the Chapayev troops in the audience to defend their dear Sevastopol in a manner expected of them.

One after another stood up the representatives of our units and sub-units, reassuring the divisional command element that they were determined to fight to the death, if necessary, to defend the approaches to Sevastopol. Among them was Pavel Morozov, commander of our platoon. After approaching the podium, Morozov bent over and scooped up a handful of earth. Then, treating it as a priceless treasure, he showed it to the audience and said: "We defended this soil against the Interventionists during the Civil War. For this soil, we, the older generation of soldiers, and our sons and daughters alongside us, shall fight to the last drop of blood." The speakers were quite reticent; indeed, it was not the time for long-winded speeches. However, each and every one of us mentally swore to fulfil our duty.

A tiresome German twin-fuselage spy plane hung in the sky from the early morning until twilight. Having dropped their load on Sevastopol, Nazi bombers did not miss the battle zone, either. Returning to their home bases, they flew at treetop level over communication trenches, strafing them with their machine guns and dropping propaganda leaflets, the contents of which made us even more mad than the bullets did.

The regimental scouts went out to reconnoitre with ever greater frequency. Our nighttime reconnaissance-in-force engaged the enemy periodically, to evoke a reaction from the thoroughly camouflaged enemy firing points. Using anti-tank grenades, our lads managed to discover and destroy several enemy machine-gun clusters that were inaccessible to our artillery, because they were hidden in rocks and under rock overhangs.

The scouts kept bringing alarming news from behind German lines. The Nazis kept saturating their positions with artillery ever more densely, and more and more of their tanks and self-propelled guns were accumulating around us. A period of new fierce battles was drawing near.

Again bloody blisters appeared on the hands of Sevastopol's defenders. With a great deal of effort, we deepened our trenches in the stony soil, centimetre after centimetre. We cut down trees and branches, which we used to camouflage our dugouts and permanent strong points. We gouged out new, alternate entrenchments. It was hot and there was not enough water.

And then it started. Morozov jumped into our permanent strong point. Scratching his shaved head, he said: "It looks like this is for real." The preparatory artillery bombardment was terrible. We didn't hear the separate explosions; a deafening continuous thunder rolled over the battle zone. Our pillbox rocked from side to side. Two large calibre shells exploded so close that in each case the machine gun was knocked down to the floor. It seemed that the earth itself shivered in the throes of a fever, as it were. Because of the heat, dust, and powder fumes, it became unbearably stuffy in the pillbox.

Deafened and ignoring the new, ever stronger explosions, I stood beside the embrasure, peering into the distance. I knew that the enemy artillery strike could end unexpectedly. Meanwhile, the Nazis would have had the opportunity to approach our defences under the cover of their own fire. However, I saw nothing except fire, black smoke, and the ground "reared up on its legs," as it were.

"Look out," I heard Morozov speak close to my ear. "There mustn't be any slip-ups! Not a single enemy must reach this pillbox! Meanwhile, I am going to inspect other machine-gun crews." I wanted to talk to Morozov, but he went out before I had the chance to do it. "Actually," I consoled myself, "there are log emplacements in the company that are much more vulnerable than our pillbox!" As if divining my thoughts, Samarskiy shouted: "Don't worry; we'll manage!" I nodded in agreement.

Then Olya Tkachenko paid us a visit. She inquired whether there were wounded amongst us. "Everyone is fine," Samarskiy said cheerfully. I couldn't resist asking her how many wounded there were so far in our sub-unit. Olya's reaction was to give up as hopeless. Though she experienced a bombardment of such magnitude for the first time, she behaved magnificently.

Olya's husband Fedor also dropped in on us. "Why don't you stay put? You promised me not to take risks!" Olya reprimanded him.

"You promised the same thing to me," he replied in a good-natured manner.

"The wounded need me."

"And I must attend to the able-bodied, which is even more important!"

They smiled at each other and went about their business.

In about an hour, the artillery and mortar fire began to quiet down noticeably. The single explosions of heavy, long-range shells were distinctly heard through the intermittent thunder. Then gaps, as it were, appeared in the overall din. In the end came the final explosions of shells and mortar bombs. Even after it was all over, the buzzing and humming in my head continued, my ears were ringing, and when I attempted to get up to take a step, everything began to swim and rock all around. A thick dust slowly settled in the hot air, saturated with powder fumes. First the sun came out, becoming clearly visible, and then the blue sky appeared.

Grown haggard and seeming older, Morozov dropped into the pillbox for the umpteenth time. Having wiped the sweat off his forehead, he shook his empty flask, squeezed his submachine gun, slipped out to the surface, and began to examine the approaches to our defensive line. Charred and split stumps were all that remained where trees recently had stood. The grass was burnt completely, and smoke still issued from the craters. No camouflage of any kind remained on our positions.

The enemy infantry had not yet arrived and the ground was gradually becoming enveloped by an impenetrable silence. However, this silence was short-lived; a distant roar was heard in the sky as the enemy aircraft approached us. "As if we haven't had enough already," Morozov muttered, hastily rolling a cigarette, in order to have a smoke before the bombing started. When he saw that a soldier named Kurbatov was leaving his cover, he shouted in a hoarse voice: "Air!"

"Air! Air!" the observers joined in.

With the hand-rolled cigarette between his teeth, Morozov raised his head and kept looking for some time at the swiftly approaching black dots, which gradually turned into little lines. Then he began to count the aircraft aloud. When he counted sixty, he took out the now extinguished cigarette from his mouth and spat out: "Does it really matter how many of them come? We'll fire at them, hiding from the bomb splinters, but obviously there is no escape in the battle zone from a direct hit of an aerial bomb."

Our miraculously preserved anti-aircraft guns opened up, but the high-flying bombers were out of their range. "They went past us," remarked Kurbatov with a sigh of relief, turning to Olya Tkachenko standing nearby.

"Are you pleased?" demanded Olya, looking into Kurbatov's eyes angrily. Nodding in the direction of the city, she asked: "What about them?"

Kurbatov failed to reply.

"Air! Air!" the observers shouted again.

This time the aircraft approached us downsun, so they were difficult to see and count. About fifty of them formed a "devil's wheel," to avoid getting into each other's way. Then they began to dive at us. It seemed to me that the very earth howled in fear of the striking bombs. Blinking nervously, you closed your eyes and your shaking body huddled up and involuntarily hugged the stony ground.

Though a thundering death fell from the sky, you had to muster enough moral strength during this hell to go into an open trench and fire at the enemy aircraft. "Two aircraft!" yelled Kurbatov, grabbing Morozov by his shoulders. "Flying directly at us. Two aircraft!" Unperturbed, Morozov bent over an anti-tank weapon, readying it for use. "Why are you screaming?" he demanded. "You think I am blind? Better stand by your machine gun, son. As you are firing, take a good aim and make sure that you don't overshoot."

Then a number of bombs fell, gouging the ground right beside the trench.

Kurbatov forced himself to get up, after placing to one side the loaded magazines of his captured light machine gun. He pulled out the machine gun, half covered with earth, from a recess, blew its barrel through, wiped it with a clean cloth, placed it directly on the parapet, and readied it for firing. There was no place to hide; the Nazi pilots had thoroughly reconnoitred our positions. Having dropped their bombs, the first bomber wave strafed our trenches with machine-gun fire. We returned their fire with rifles and automatic weapons.

Then Morozov proved successful in putting an armour-piercing bullet directly into the belly of one Junkers as it was recovering from a dive. The Junkers began to sway like a wounded bird, attempted to climb, and came down behind the German trenches. We screamed and laughed from joy, but a new raid forced us all to mind our business. Morozov took aim at another plane marked with a swastika, but held his fire when he saw that the plane was already burning and falling to the ground like a stone. Finally, the third Junkers knocked out by our platoon blew itself up by its own bombs after landing.

Even a raid as fierce as this must eventually end. After it was finished, we began to get ready to receive Nazi infantry. "Tell me who shot down the last plane?" Fedor Tkachenko inquired of a middle-aged soldier who slowly rolled a thin cigarette.

"How can you tell, Comrade Political Instructor? Maybe it was me, and maybe it was him," the soldier said, nodding toward Kurbatov. "After you fire a bullet, you don't see it in the sky. You don't know whether it went into thin air or into the aircraft you aimed at. We all fired at the same planes. One was shot down by Junior Lieutenant Morozov. As for the other two.... Well, I don't know."

"Does this mean that nobody is to be recommended for decorations, for shooting them down?"

The soldier gave Tkachenko a surprised look. "What do you mean —nobody? What about Colonel Nikolay Vasil'yevich Zakharov, who commanded our regiment until recently. He had trained us, and we owe him a great deal. So he should be the one to be honoured!"

"They are coming!" someone shouted. The Nazi soldiers went into the attack. At first they approached us by short bounds. We kept quiet, so they became emboldened.

I pressed myself against the embrasure, looking at the patch of land disfigured by craters in front of our pillbox. I looked at it and didn't recognize it, as I couldn't find a single even barely noticeable mound of earth with a mine in it. The entire space in front of our line was cleared of the mines our engineers had laid. (We were relying on these mines to some extent to keep the Germans away.) So I realized why a second explosion was often heard along with that of an enemy shell; these explosions also detonated our mines.

Peering into the notch of the sight, I saw the extended lines of enemy soldiers quickly climbing the slope, and I imagined that any one of them could have been the killer of Nina Onilova. Since the Germans didn't hear a single shot fired from our side and have not lost a single soldier after covering half of the way, they drew themselves to their full height and advanced toward our lines upright.

I was nervous and the palms of my hands became wet with sweat. "Well...what are you waiting for?" Samarskiy, my No. 2, whispered.

"Let's wait a minute...."

"Half a minute is enough!"

"There is still time..."

"They'll throw grenades at us!" protested Samarskiy, worried. "Make sure you're not too late!"

Submachine guns and rifles opened up on our left flank. As the Germans shifted to the right, closer to our pillbox, advancing in a tighter group, I raised the safety catch and pressed the firing lever; the Maxim let out a lengthy burst. However, subsequently I fired short bursts. I saw that I didn't miss and the bullets kept finding their marks. The thinned out extended line retreated. A second one followed, but it, too, was forced to roll back. Suddenly, I saw two Nazis armed with grenades—quite near and in our dead zone—crawling up to the pillbox.

"Tolya!" I shouted, but Samarskiy had also become aware of the mortal danger threatening us, so he dashed toward the alternate embrasure and flung a grenade through it. I took a careful look through the embrasure and saw that the German soldiers who had stealed up to our pillbox were dead.

A new attack began, and I couldn't distinguish the springy sound of the neighbouring Maxim against the background of the rifle and submachine-gun fire. I listened attentively; the second heavy machine gun, placed on the left flank, was indeed silent. I did not yet know that the Germans had destroyed the log emplacement on the left flank and Morozov, who had miraculously survived, picked up a submachine gun and went to ground in an extended line. But I was very much aware that the Germans who were going up the slope of the ravine, approaching our pillbox closer and closer, couldn't be seen from the left flank.

Now that our situation was becoming very difficult, Samarskiy ceased to be nervous. Calmly and without any haste, he wiped off the dust from the machine gun breech casing's top plate, adjusted the ammunition belt, and gave me a questioning look, as if saying: "Are you waiting again?"

I nodded and then and there opened fire. The enemy extended line was mowed down, as it were. The second line, moving behind the first one, pressed close to the ground and began to return fire with submachine guns. Bullets started to knock against the cover of the pillbox.

I paused. The second enemy extended line was followed by two additional ones. A tall German officer drew himself up to his full height and turned toward his men, shouting an order and waving his parabellum gun. A well-aimed bullet, fired by one of our men, knocked him down. Staggering, the officer discharged his gun, hitting his own soldiers; then he fell face down, rolling along the embankment into the ravine. The soldiers, as if still led by the officer, also rushed downward.

The fighting lasted less than an hour. No doubt the Germans count-ed on the results of their preparatory fire. Having gained no ground, they kept to themselves for a while.

I was so tired I had to sit down. "What happened on the left flank?" asked Samarskiy. "All right, I am going to take a look," I offered. It took a great deal of effort on my part to force myself to get up. I shoved band-ages into all of my pockets and went out.

I discovered that the log emplacement on the left flank had col-lapsed. However, from that direction came the sound of someone talking to himself in a quiet voice. I cleared a passage for myself with difficulty and squeezed inside the emplacement. A delirious soldier, wounded in both legs, muttered there to himself. After examining his dressings already soaked through with blood, I placed the wounded man in a more comfortable position, pushed a folded raincape under his head, and rushed back to my pillbox. A new enemy artillery strike had begun, so it became possible for German infantrymen to approach our pillbox very closely under the cover of their own fire.

After a while, Olya Tkachenko dropped in, complaining that she had no water for her wounded, so Samarskiy and I gave her our half-empty flasks. Soon after walked in Morozov with a bandaged head. "Is the purpose of your visit to obtain water?" he asked Olya in a stern voice.

"Yes, indeed.... Only I didn't touch the Maxim's portion. The machine gunners gave me their flasks," said Tkachenko, leaving.

"Well, how are you, my children — all in one piece?" inquired Moro-zov, approaching the machine gun. He looked it over quickly, and then glanced at Samarskiy and me, saying: "Thank God, you're alive." Our commander wiped perspiration of his face, as it was very stuffy in the pillbox. "I couldn't drop in on you during the fighting," he explained. "Those on the other flank had a very bad time."

"I know," I replied.

"Have you been there already?"

"I went to find out if I could be of any help."

"You're so smart..." said Morozov with a sad smile. "There isn't much one can do now, though; the left flank is exposed. However, I heard you firing all the time, so I didn't worry. How many rounds have you expended?"

"Two ammunition belts or five hundred rounds," I replied.

"The wench has gone mad!" exclaimed Morozov. "Well! Well!" He looked into the embrasure, examining the slope of the ravine where the corpses of Nazi soldiers had piled up. Something bothered him (perhaps the quantity of ammunition I had expended), and he turned to me: "I'll forgive you this time, but look out, Comrade Junior Sergeant, the next time I'll skin you alive. Well, all right. In case you must get in touch with me, I'll be with the Senior Sergeant Zaytsev's crew. He needs me more, since his machine gunner had been seriously wounded."

We repulsed another attack. Then the enemy artillery strike was repeated. It was around this time that Fedor and Olya Tkachenko were both killed.

I am not superstitious. However, when Samarskiy, during a short break, suddenly asked me whether I would write to him in the event something happened to me, I lost my temper in earnest. Very shortly afterwards, a yellow fountain of fire shot up beside our machine gun, and I was submerged in a strange, ringing fog. (I learned what had happened later on that day from comrades, after I was taken to the medical battalion, so I am basing myself on their testimony in continuing this story.)

* * *

Following the second artillery strike, German tanks began to advance toward the tactical line of Chapayev troops. A wall of defensive fire went up in front of the Germans, but they stubbornly pushed forward through the fire. As a result, several of the enemy tanks managed to break through to our trenches, with intoxicated infantrymen advancing behind the tanks. In addition, enemy artillery bombarded our troops from time to time. While the survivors among our Chapayev troops prepared for the upcoming engagement, Samusev suffered a severe concussion, so he turned the company over to Zaytsev.

As the tanks kept approaching our troops, their turrets, machine guns, and white-bordered crosses became more and more distinct. The troops decided to let the tanks come even closer—to a distance approximately equal to a hand grenade range—so that they could aim better. Stopping the tanks was easier said than done.... A tiny anti-tank gun challenged to a duel ten tanks, huge machines made of steel. Its crew, commanded by Senior Lieutenant Fokin, battery commander, fired over open sights. The duel lasted only a few minutes. After it was over, three enemy tanks, enveloped with flames and acrid smoke, were burning beside our trench. Then, a fourth one wriggled out from behind this smoke screen, stopped, and took accurate aim. The anti-tank gun was thrown to one side and nobody of the gun detachment survived.

It was then that Zaytsev jumped onto the parapet and threw a grenade under the bottom of the tank. A fountain of red and black flames shot out from under the torn off hatch cover. Afterwards, Zaytsev stood still for a while, looking at the tank, as if trying to convince himself that it was really immobilized. Weary, he wiped perspiration off his face. The rest of the tanks turned back and enemy infantry swerved to the right, so as not to fall under their own tanks. Then and there, Anatoliy Samarskiy unbosomed himself. Since firing through the embrasure limited his arc of fire, he dragged the machine gun out of the pillbox with the aid of a comrade, and duly settled his accounts with the retreating German soldiers.

* * *

"Our unlucky Zoya, the poor thing, has already landed in the medical battalion," said Ivanova, about to sit down beside Samarskiy on the ground. "Are you telling me that she promised to write to you? Well, then, she will write; she always keeps her promises." Samarskiy's face kept getting darker and darker. To change the subject, Masha asked Anatoliy why he maintained that only the two of them remained in the battle zone out of the entire company. "There are seven of us. I know for sure," she insisted.

"The other five are new recruits," said Samarskiy, giving up as hopeless. "They had never been under fire." Samarskiy and Ivanova stopped talking for a while. Then the three sentries who had just been relieved joined them. The soldiers removed their submachine guns and laid them down on the ground.

A stuffy southern night covered the trenches snugly. It seemed that a huge sack made of matting had been thrown over the entire world; through the loosely-woven fabric only the twinkling, low stars and bright streaks made by tracer bullets showed here and there. From time to time, the ringing silence was broken by the dreary sound of a machine gun blazing away, and then the frightened echo kept rushing about in the ravine.

"Well, guys, what else is there to do?" asked one of the new recruits. "Let us wait for the messenger [that had been sent to the battalion HQ—Trans.]," replied another one. "Perhaps he will bring us an order from the HQ."

"Let us wait," agreed Samarskiy, even though he was not convinced the messenger would ever come back. However, in a few minutes the silhouette of the messenger emerged from the darkness. "Well, speak of the devil!" said Samarskiy, relieved, though he couldn't help sounding reproachful. "I had to wait for the Captain," the messenger replied in a tired voice. Then he added: "The battalion commander ordered us to retreat." Samarskiy raised himself on one elbow, asking: "How can we retreat?"

"Very simply, by using our feet...." The messenger unbuttoned a pocket of his field shirt, took out a packet wrapped in a newspaper, and handed it to Samarskiy. "Here, take it and read it."

"And read it I will!" replied Samarskiy in an unexpectedly angry voice. "What's there to read!" He took the packet and went down into a trench. Having covered himself with a raincape, he began to read, by the light of a match, the message written on a sheet torn out from an exercise book. He recognized the Captain's handwriting. The messenger told them the truth; the battalion commander indeed ordered them to retreat.

When Samarskiy, his heart heavy, returned to the comrades waiting for him, Ivanova told him the joyful news: "Political Instructor Sergeyev has joined us!"

"That's great!" exclaimed Samarskiy, becoming animated. He had known the Political Instructor [formerly, Komsomol Organizer of the regiment—Trans.] for some time, and realized immediately that Sergeyev's timely appearance would likely have a good effect on the morale of the survivors among our Chapayev troops, who were perturbed and dispirited. "And how long are you planning to stay with us, Comrade Political Instructor?" he asked.

"I am here for good," Sergeyev replied simply. He sat down on a boulder. Cautiously illuminating a sheet of paper with a flashlight, he hastily jotted down a few words on it; then he handed the folded sheet to Samarskiy, ordering him to deliver it to the battalion commander.

"Why are you sending me away, Comrade Political Instructor?"

"It's an order," Sergeyev stated firmly.

"Yes, Sir!" replied Samarskiy and left.

After Samarskiy had gone, the submachine-gun fire in our company's sector heated up again, for the Nazis mounted another attack, attempting to capture straight off the trenches defended by a handful of Chapayev troops. The bloody skirmish lasted for more than an hour. The enemy failed to withstand our resistance and was rolled back, but the victory cost us dearly; of the entire company, the only survivors were Ivanova and Sergeyev, the latter of whom had been badly wounded.

After locating him with great difficulty at the bottom of a dark trench, Ivanova, herself wounded in the shoulder and straining every muscle, dragged Sergeyev in the direction where she believed were the main elements of our battalion.

"Leave me behind, Masha," Sergeyev whispered when he regained consciousness during a short halt. "Just give me one grenade and then go." But Ivanova refused. Biting her lip to master the pain in her injured shoulder, she continued to drag the wounded man. At dawn, when the last stars went out in the sky and the ground, all covered with craters, had become visible, she finally reached friendly troops. After handing Sergeyev over to medical orderlies and quickly bandaging her own wound, she decided to return to the battle zone. The commanding officer of our regiment intervened at this point and ordered that she be evacuated to the Inkerman Caves, the temporary location of our medical battalion.

On the way to the Caves, the truck in which Ivanova travelled was attacked by several Messerschmitts. She and Sergeyev—whom she covered with her body—were both wounded, in the head and abdomen respectively. The driver was wounded as well, but managed to reach a military unit, and from there the wounded were delivered to an evacuation hospital.

It was my third day in the medical battalion and I was considered an "old-timer." I don't know how I would have coped with a concussion and an eye wound in peacetime, but there, in the fighting Sevastopol, I had barely come to when I got up; and I wasn't the only one to do so.

A short June night was about to end, and the truck which was to bring wounded personnel had not yet returned from the battle zone. This gave rise to various rumours in the Caves. Some of the soldiers speculated that there were no new casualties, due to a lull in the fighting. Others believed that our regiment had been surrounded, and it wouldn't be easy to break out of the encirclement even for those who were of sound body and mind.... To the majority of us, the second alternative seemed more plausible than the first. However, we needed a confirmation to this effect, so I approached Sergey Ivanovich Zudin, our regimental commanding officer's deputy in charge of logistics. The reception he gave me instantly convinced me that our situation was very bad indeed. Nevertheless, I ventured a question: "Sergey Ivanovich, do you know why the truck with the wounded personnel hasn't yet returned?"

"I don't know. I haven't been told," Zudin replied. Apparently, the old soldier was reluctant to tell me the bitter truth. In fact, our regiment had been encircled, and it was highly unlikely that the truck sent to the battle zone to pick up our wounded personnel would ever come back.

"Well?" I was questioned by Senior Sergeant Zarya, a spokesman for a group of convalescents anxious to return to the front. I gave up as hopeless. "Obviously," Zarya summed up the situation, "we are not going to wait for special instructions. And we are not going to wait until transportation is arranged for us, either. By this evening, we'll reach the battle zone on foot." His plan met with universal approval. We were ready in no time. After we had packed our kit-bags and were resting for a while before setting off, Zarya picked up a forgotten guitar from a table, plucked the strings, and began to sing very quietly:

> Our native sea lies behind us,
> And shells are exploding all around.
> Smoke rises from the city in ruins,
> The enemy is closing the ring.

This song was written by an unknown author during the fighting for Sevastopol, and both seamen and infantrymen loved it equally. Listening to the simple, courage inspiring lyrics, I mentally returned to my comrades-in-arms at the front:

> Outnumbered, we'll perish; so be it!
> But our brothers will gain victory.
> They'll reclaim our native land
> And square accounts with the enemy in full.

Zarya struck the final chord and then pressed the palm of his right hand against the strings. "That's enough!" he said and strode toward the exit from the Caves with his kit-bag thrown over one shoulder.

We walked along the burnt ground, ploughed again and again by bombs and shells, until evening. Finally, we heard the distant rapping of a heavy machine gun. Even though I knew that the "ta-ta-ta" beat of all machine guns sounds the same, I grabbed Zarya by one sleeve, exclaiming involuntarily: "Do you hear my 'Maksimka?' Honestly, it's mine!"

"Ah!" Zarya retorted contemptuously. "Just you try to identify it.... You would think your Maxim was the only one in the battle zone!"

When we reached the road which previously led to the regimental HQ, it was already dark. We hadn't even had time to make ten steps when one after another malevolent submachine-gun bursts began to fall almost beside us. "Turn back!" an angry voice came from behind us. Going to ground, I managed to notice a soldier with a machine gun to the right of me. "Hell, where do you think you're going?" He opened his eyes wide when Zarya and I crawled up to him. "Strait into the Nazi clutches!"

"We are on our way to the regimental HQ," explained Zarya. "We belong to the Chapayev Division—get it?"

"All of us here are Chapayev troops," replied the machine gunner. "But your people are no longer at the old location. Now Hitler's youth keeps going into attacks against us from there."

"Whose man are you?" I asked. "Zhidilov's—that's whose!" explained the machine gunner, turning back the collar of his field shirt and revealing a striped sailor's vest. So that's who he was! I immediately recalled a rainy spring day when I slipped and fell into the mud, right in front of a dark-complexioned, skinny colonel, surrounded by marines. The colonel helped me to get up and advised me to watch my step in the future. "Who was he?" I asked one of the marines later on. He looked me over with amazement and replied, hardly hiding his contempt: "Eh, you infantry!" After a moment of silence he added in a completely different tone: "It was Zhidilov, infantry!"

Heavy mortar bombs began to explode all around. There was no doubt: the Germans were mounting an attack. "Come, sister, adjust the belt" the marine shouted, clinging to his machine gun, and opened fire at the dark silhouettes flashing among the bushes. But I was not fated to adjust his ammunition belt for very long; unexpectedly, the marine's head drooped and his machine gun was silenced.

"Volodya, take a look!" I turned to Zarya, grabbing the machine gun's carrying handles. Since receiving my wound, I've been having problems with my eyesight. Perpetual darkness stood in my right eye, while bright spots floated in front of the left one. I began to fire, with Zarya giving me aiming instructions from time to time. By the multiple howl that came from the bushes I guessed that my bullets have been finding their mark, and I wholeheartedly rejoiced at this. "Well done, Zoya," I heard Zarya speak, from a distance as it were. "Only aim more to the left!" he shout-ed, adjusting the dusty belt with his bloodied hands. Finally, he banged the top cover of the breech casing with the palm of his hand. "That's enough! Or else, instead of the Fritzes, we mow down our own mari-nes!" Indeed, a united "hurrah" came from the left, where silhouettes in striped sailor's vests flashed. "Look at them"—half critically and half ad-miringly remarked Zarya—"they are fighting in their striped sailor's vests alone!"

After the enemy attack had bogged down, Zarya hopefully peered at the scorched bushes for some time. "No.... Our people are nowhere to be seen," he said in the end. "So you better go back," said a stranger, adjusting a wrinkled and soiled field service cap on his bandaged head. Zarya gave him an angry look, and without responding went to get his kit-bag which he had temporarily abandoned.

Dusk was falling quickly. The exchange of fire kept quieting down more and more noticeably. Zarya returned, shaking his kit-bag pierced by shell fragments. "And now, my one-eyed machine gunner, let's have something to eat," he offered, reaching for a can of fish and two pieces of dry wheat bread, hard as a rock. "Otherwise we'll arrive hungry in the next world, should we get killed," he added.

"Why did you call me 'one-eyed?'" I asked Zarya reproachfully. "You can't fool me," he replied. "After all, you depended on my instructions." I refused to eat, and decided to look for the missing machine-gun crew. "Don't bother," Zarya tried to dissuade me. "The machine gun is not a needle in a haystack. The crew will claim it sooner or later; that is, if they are still alive."

He was right. We had barely laid out the food, when we heard a crackling noise and a stranger emerged from the bushes, carrying an ammunition box. "Listen brother," he addressed me. "I am looking for our machine gun. Have you seen it, by any chance?"

"Here it is," I reassured him.

"Excuse me; I took you for a man in the dark. Young girl, have you seen my friend Vanya?"

"Your friend is dead," I said quietly and got up to show the marine where his dead friend lay. Suddenly, several shells exploded nearby....

A sharp pain in my head caused me to wake up. I realized that someone was turning inside out the pockets of my field shirt, looking for my identification papers. I had the urge to shout: "Don't touch, I am alive!" But I was only able to let out a quiet moan.

"She is alive, after all," I heard someone saying. I was conscious of being lifted and carried. I again blacked out on the way, and when I came to I became aware of the sound of screw propellers operating at full capacity. Then I began to feel seasick from the roll and realized I was aboard a ship. Afterwards, anti-aircraft guns fired frequently, bombs fell with a booming sound into the sea, and the ship kept executing evasive manoeuvres, now to one side and now to the other, trying to avoid a direct hit.

Suddenly, it was quiet, the silence being interrupted by moans and water splashing behind the thin bulkhead. "We've arrived," I heard a wounded man saying. "That's right," confirmed a seaman sitting beside him. "Safe and sound," as they say. The wounded man began to question him excitedly: "Tell us where we are going! How long will they keep us there?"

"We've arrived in Sochi, guys," the seaman reassured the passengers. "No need to get excited; better begin gathering your belongings slowly." To prevent a delay in the disembarkation of seriously wounded personnel, those who were mobile were told to assemble on the upper deck and come ashore without a special order. As I stopped on the gangway to allow two medical orderlies carrying a stretcher pass, the wounded man on it exclaimed: "Zoya! You are alive!" The voice was familiar to me; it was Senior Sergeant Volodya Zarya.

CHAPTER III

THE HOSPITAL

Less than a year earlier I passed through Sochi at night, on our way to Odessa, but I have never seen it in daytime. I had been told repeatedly what a lovely town it was, and remember that Sochi also seemed very beautiful to my fellow wounded when we arrived there to be hospitalized. Myself hindered by my impaired vision, I learned from comments made by those around me that there were luxuriant trees growing in a carefree manner, that the sea rolled calmly beside the shore, and that bold, black-beaked sea gulls floated on the waves. I tried to visualize the beauty of all this and couldn't.

After disembarking from the ship, on the shore we boarded buses which travelled along a smooth road with poplars growing on both sides. The road had many turns, and the bus was rocking. Every jolt caused me pain. Leaning against the soft back of the seat, I closed my eyes and promptly fell asleep. When I woke up, our bus stood beside a magnificent building with columns. One of my fellow-passengers informed us that this was a former sanatorium, but now the building housed a military hospital.

I was the last to get off the bus. The nurse who received the wounded lost her composure somewhat when she saw a woman in front of her. Then she asked me kindly what was the matter with my eye. Supporting me carefully, she led me into a hospital room and seated me gently on the bed, saying: "Now you are home, as it were. Here is your gown and slippers. Please change. By the way, what is your name?"

"Zoya," I replied to the nurse, a very young and chubby redhead.

"You are my namesake! Well, I must run; I have to take other patients to their beds," she told me. Left all alone, I tried to make some sense of the events of the previous twenty-four hours. Now I saw the head of the marine/machine gunner with a bullet through it, now the cheerful Zarya smiled at me from under his bandages, and now I suddenly heard the deafening cracking of the exploding shells. However, most of all I was concerned about my vision. I was afraid to admit, even to myself, that I was almost blind. Darkness stood in my wounded eye; and though I could distinguish objects with the other one, for some reason they were covered by a patch of white mildew. The thought that

I was maimed for life kept tormenting me. I couldn't stand it, so I buried my head in the pillow and began to sob.

The nurse Zoya dropped into my room in the late afternoon. "What's the matter with you?" she asked, alarmed.

"Never mind. Don't pay any attention to me."

"Never mind, you say, and you cried so much that your pillow is completely drenched," said Zoya, and sat down on my bed. "You mustn't."

I was touched. "I simply am very silly," I admitted and smiled at her through my tears.

My roommate happened to be a sympathetic dark-haired young girl, called Anya. I introduced myself to her the next morning and immediately learned that Anya considered herself to be completely recovered, so for some time she had been trying to obtain discharge from the hospital.

Time passed. My vision failed to improve, but I didn't complain. I lay in bed practically all the time, indifferently looking at the ceiling, and kept thinking and thinking....

One evening, Zoya came in and said, turning to my roommate: "At long last, your wish is about to come true; soon you'll be discharged."

"Are you serious?"

"Of course. We ought to keep you longer, but we need your bed, since another group of wounded is about to arrive," the nurse explained. Anya began to jump for joy and immediately started to pack her meagre belongings. Almost nobody slept at the hospital that night, since everyone was waiting for daybreak and the arrival of the new wounded. Everyone was anxious to learn the news from the front as soon as possible.

Immediately following the morning rounds, somebody knocked quietly on our door. "May I?" he asked in a deep voice. When he entered, I couldn't discern the features of the face but the voice was quite familiar.

"Who is this?" I asked, excitedly.

"Hello, Zoya! Don't you recognize me? It's Kozhevnikov."

"Oh, my goodness! It's Vasya! Sit down and tell me the news! How are our friends; have you met any of our acquaintances here?"

"Samusev is here."

"Really?"

"He was concussed. He shakes, is deaf, and can hardly talk."

"What about you?"

"I am doing fine; I heal like a dog. However, I don't know what to do with our commander. He doesn't want to eat and drink. He doesn't want to write home. 'I am of no use to anyone; I am a cripple,' he says."

"How can he talk like that!"

"What can I do?" Kozhevnikov threw up his hands. "I begged him and I swore at him, but it's no use."

"You men are silly," Anya intervened. "Where is your Samusev? Let me talk to him."

"Well, maybe it will work!" Kozhevnikov livened up. "What do you think, Zoya?"

"There is no time to think!" interrupted Anya. "We must act." She jumped off her bed, grabbed Kozhevnikov's hand, and almost dragged him to the door.

She returned triumphant. "Here it is!" she exclaimed, raising over her head a triangular wartime letter, carefully glued together.

"He did write it, after all!" I exclaimed joyfully.

"I don't take 'no' for an answer. I am going to take the letter to the nurse."

On that very same day, Kozhevnikov and I had an unpleasant experience. A very young soldier with a bandaged face was brought in by bus. Supported by a nurse, he got out of the bus and, listening to the exclamations of those who came to meet the bus, he asked in a loud voice: "Are there any Chapayev troops here? I am Sizov, Private Sizov, a scout," the soldier identified himself.

"Kolya!" Kozhevnikov and I exclaimed in unison, rushing toward the wounded man. "Kolya, my friend," muttered Kozhevnikov, hugging his fellow countryman. "So we've again run into each other, after all!"

"Vasya, is this you?" the soldier asked, carefully feeling the face, shoulders, and chest of Kozhevnikov with his shaking fingers.

"Yes, yes, it's me; don't get upset."

"I am dying for a smoke, my fellow countryman."

"In a second!" Kozhevnikov led Sizov to a bench, seated him, and began to roll a cigarette for him hurriedly. He lit it and passed it to Sizov, who inhaled deeply.

We were very tempted—but did not dare—to pry Sizov with questions about the situation at the front, to find out what fate befell our comrades-in-arms. As if divining our thoughts, Sizov took out the cigarette from his mouth and said: "Sevastopol will fall any day now...."

"Nonsense!" Kozhevnikov interrupted him. "Who says this?"

"Everybody," Sizov replied drily, deeply offended.

Around this time, Kozhevnikov and I on several occasions had shared our fears as to the outcome of the fighting for Sevastopol. All the same, Sizov's statement now seemed sacrilegious to us. The three of us ceased talking, and were thinking about the same thing.

"Let's go," I said finally, touching Kozhevnikov's shoulder. We slipped our hands under Sizov's arms and led him toward the building.

When I returned to my room, I found Anya crying; we were not the only ones to learn about the true situation at the front. When she saw me, Anya began to walk toward me, saying: "Well, Zoyka, I am leaving...." Only then, as Anya stood before me, I noticed that she was wearing a uniform and that the red enamel of the Order of the Red Star shone on her chest.

I didn't want to pry her with questions. I knew that the hospital granted Anya a ten-day leave, but looking at her I realized that she was not going to use it.

Kozhevnikov came in the evening, as usual. He was very excited.

"What happened?"

"You see, Zoya.... I have some news, but I don't know whether I should believe it or not. They say Masha is here in the hospital."

"Ivanova?"

"Who else? I found this out from a friend I met here. Supposedly, she is in the surgical ward."

I knew that for some time our hero scout has not been indifferent toward my friend. Looking at his strong hands crushing a towel at the head of the bed, I realized that Kozhevnikov wanted me to help him.

"Let's go," I said, asking no more questions.

We wandered along the corridors in the surgical ward for a long time, until we were shown the room in which one Ivanova lay. Pale and silent, Kozhevnikov gently knocked on the door.

When Masha saw us, she tried to get up, but her arms and legs refused to obey her. "Mashen'ka!" I rushed toward her. "You've survived, my dear...."

"I am fine," whispered Masha, burying her happy face in my bosom and suddenly burst into tears.

"Oh, you females," reacted Kozhevnikov, speaking in an unnaturally cheerful voice. "You must have a good cry!"

I silently shook a finger at him.

"Well, that's enough; stop it," I said, trying to calm Masha down. "My dear, dear friends!" she said, after she stopped crying. "If you only knew how happy I am to see you! I've been lying here alone, days at a time. It is so quiet and scary. Sometimes I have the urge to scream...."

"How long have you been here?" asked Kozhevnikov.

"Already ten days. Do sit down, Vasya," insisted Masha. "I can't look at you when you are pacing the floor—my head is spinning."

"Ten days! And we didn't even know you were here all this time. We found you, thanks to Kozhevnikov." I nodded toward him. "He deserves all the credit for locating you."

The conversation gradually shifted to the subject that was constantly on our minds. We talked about Sevastopol and reminisced about our regiment. We mentioned those who were alive and remembered the dead.

"This means that there is five of us here," Kozhevnikov calculated.

"And who else is here?" asked Masha.

"Samusev and Kolya Sizov."

"How are they?"

"In bad shape," Kozhevnikov said, sighing. "Nikolay is blind and Samusev will never fight again, I am afraid. By the way, I've almost forgotten to tell you he received a letter today."

"He should be grateful to Anya! Without her, he would still be lying in bed, feeling sorry for himself."

"Don't be too hard on him, Zoya," reacted Kozhevnikov. "The man was truly desperate. Of course, he is now angry at himself, but he couldn't have helped behaving the way he did.... As for Kol'ka, he is the one I am now concerned about. He is so distressed...."

"Oh, Vasya, we must look after him," said Masha, letting out a sob.

"I do look after him."

"But you've left him alone to join us."

"He was asleep, so I felt I could leave him for a while."

When Kozhevnikov returned to their room, he found Sizov awake and unable to go back to sleep. "What's with you, Kolya? Do you need anything?" he asked, concerned.

"Vasya, Vasya," repeated Sizov ignoring Kozhevnikov's question. "Do sit down beside me. I know that you're going to ask to be discharged soon. So do me a favour, my friend, and wait awhile. Will you? Perhaps this delay will give me time to become accustomed to the idea that soon you'll leave me behind...."

"I'll wait awhile, Kolya. I promise."

So the two fellow countrymen spent the whole night sitting up and talking.

* * *

After Major M.S. Antipin, the new commanding officer of our regiment, was wounded, Major B.A. Shestopalov, his chief of staff, replaced him.

Following a three days' rest, the regiment again moved into action. Early in the morning of the first day of fighting, Shestopalov set out for the positions occupied by the battalion commanded by Senior Lieutenant Rybal'chenko (who took over the command of the battalion during the heavy June fighting when many officers were put out of action; he had been deputy chief of staff of our regiment). The battalion's positions, Major Shestopalov believed, were the most vulnerable ones in the entire regiment. Though the battalion lacked one-third of its strength, other subunits also found themselves in a similar predicament. What really worried the Major was Rybal'chenko's youth and inexperience.

When Shestopalov arrived in the battalion disposition, Rybal'chenko happened to be absent from the battalion HQ; Shestopalov found him on the left flank, in a company which had borne the brunt of the enemy offensive. Armed with a submachine gun, Rybal'chenko led the troops in repelling yet another enemy attack. When Shestopalov saw the company commander's body, covered with a greatcoat, in the company HQ, he immediately realized why Rybal'chenko chose to be with this particular company; the new battalion commander's perception of his place in battle was absolutely correct. In turn, when he saw Shestopalov, Rybal'chenko immediately guessed the real reason for his superior's visit. Therefore, when Shestopalov sincerely praised him at the end of the day, Rybal'chenko, his eyes bloodshot from lack of sleep, merely smiled at him condescendingly.

It was already dark when Shestopalov returned to his command post. As he opened the door of the regimental HQ, he saw, by the light of a wick lamp, the broad back of Commissar Tsapenko, sitting behind the table and charging the drum magazine of a captured submachine gun.

"Well, have you had enough fighting?" he asked Shestopalov amicably.

"Up to here," replied Shestopalov, passing the edge of the palm of his hand across his throat.

"Our losses are heavy," said Tsapenko sighing. "For instance, half of Morozov's men were put out of action."

"Everyone is in the same situation," said Shestopalov, lowering himself onto the couch. He felt he ought to send somebody to Morozov as replacement for his political instructor killed during the recent fighting. As if divining his thoughts, Tsapenko told him: "Old man Morozov is certainly lucky! So many times he and his men have counterattacked, sustaining heavy losses, but he remained unscathed himself—as if he were charmed. Only I've no assistant to send him; he must do without one."

"I am in total agreement with you," replied Tsapenko.

Soon after this exchange, Senior Lieutenant Kondrat Vasil'yevich Kutsenko, chief of the regimental engineers, entered the dugout, bending almost in half. He had just returned from a reconnaissance mission. "May I report, Comrade Major?" asked Kutsenko, saluting the Major.

"Go ahead, chief of engineers," said Shestopalov, nodding in his direction. "Sit down and report." Kutsenko gave a very brief account of his reconnoitring. He was of the opinion that contact had been lost with the unit on the right flank. "It is quiet there, Comrade Major, suspiciously quiet," said Kutsenko.

Shestopalov had already guessed that there was trouble on the right flank, and Kutsenko merely confirmed his suspicions. "All right. Get some rest. Meanwhile, the Commissar and I will decide what to do...." he told Kutsenko. "Well, old man, what shall we do?" he asked, turning to Tsapenko.

"To begin with, we are out of shells, and secondly, all of our guns have been knocked out," said the Commissar counting on his fingers. "We must retreat immediately, under the cover of darkness. Otherwise, they will kill us all in the morning."

"Indeed, they will kills us all," repeated Shestopalov clenching his fists until his joints crunched, and got up resolutely. "Let's go!" he shouted. So three hundred men—the remnants of a one-time full-strength regiment —followed Major Shestopalov into the night, having left behind a weak screen made up of Kutsenko's engineers.

However, the troops marched unimpeded for only a short time; the vanguard barely entered the May Day Ravine when the Germans opened fire. Their submachine guns began blazing away on the left and right, and in a while also in the rear area, where Kutsenko and his men stayed behind.

The troops' worst fears were confirmed; their regiment was encircled. Major Shestopalov separated his men into two groups, which both made the attempt to break through simultaneously, but in two different places. For more than an hour the troops' hand grenades clanked in the dark, and in the end the Germans failed to withstand their furious onslaught; they opened the ring and let go the prey that had been almost theirs. However, a tragedy cast gloom over the troops' rejoicing; they lost their popular Commissar Grigoriy I. Tsapenko, who fell during the breakout. His body was picked up by Senior Lieutenant Kutsenko's combat engineers, who eventually caught up with the regiment, which then took up all-round defence. After mounting a guard, Shestopalov summoned Kutsenko.

"There is work to be done, Senior Lieutenant," he told his chief of combat engineers. "We must make contact with the Division. Take Samarskiy and try to break through to the Division. Should you reach your destination, report that the regiment still has one hundred bayonets at its disposal, that there are no guns, that the regimental Colours are intact, and that the men still regard themselves as a fighting unit.... Well, it's time to go. "Shestopalov gave Kutsenko an affectionate, little push. The Major had become very fond of him. While sending him on this very dangerous mission, Shestopalov realized that, in all likelihood, he will never see him again. Our regimental commanding officer himself expected to be killed that night and the prospect that he might die first, before Kutsenko, consoled him.

Both Kondrat Kutsenko and Anatoliy Samarskiy reached the divisional HQ by mid-day. They were immediately led before the divisional commanding officer. After listening to Kutsenko's report, General Kolomiyets asked the men whether they would be able to find their way back to the regiment. "We'll find it, General," Kutsenko reassured him cheerfully.

"I realize that you're tired," said the General, "and you deserve a rest. However, in light of the circumstances, it is imperative that you immediately return to your regiment. Tell Shestopalov to lead his men into Kruglaya Bay. Our ships will be waiting for them there. Have you any questions?"

"No, Comrade General," replied Kutsenko, drawing himself up.

"Well then, I wish you success. And hurry, hurry..."

However, Kutsenko was not fated to reach the regiment. It was many years after the war that I found out what had befallen him. When Kutsenko and Samarskiy reached the road, the former tried to stop a speeding truck, but was knocked down by it, receiving serious injuries. Samarskiy managed to squeeze Kutsenko into a passing ambulance. However, in a few minutes it came under heavy artillery and mortar fire. A shell exploded nearby; the ambulance caught fire and Kutsenko was thrown clear from the burning vehicle. When he came to, he overhead a conversation in German in his vicinity. He dreaded being taken prisoner, particularly in view of his serious injuries, so he tried to blow himself up with a hand grenade miraculously preserved in his pocket, but it failed to explode. Though also wounded, Samarskiy managed to reach the regiment, transmitting the General's order. However, no ships came to Kruglaya Bay....

* * *

The events described unfolded while I lay in the hospital in Sochi.

The hospital was full of smells. Ether and chloroform exuded a sharp and sweetish smell. Ichthyol and iodine gave off the aroma of resin. You smelled alcohol, sauerkraut, medications, coarse tobacco, and flowers wilting on the nightstands. At night, the silent wards became permeated by the smell of the sea and the aroma of the roses which grew beside the open windows.

The hospital was full of sounds. Thermometers clanked, the squashed ampoules crunched underfoot, the bells rang when a seriously wounded patient took a turn for the worse in a distant ward, and felt soles stamped on the floor.

Never before did reality split up for me into such a multitude of smells and sounds. Never before my sense of smell and my perception of sound were as sharp. Never before was I able to recreate, from the past, such bright and convex images—scenes in relief—on the basis of a single sign captured from the unbroken darkness. And all this happened independently of my will.

The entire world around me, even if reduced to wartime life—harsh, inexpressibly difficult, but nevertheless visible—was hidden from me by the dense, coarse-textured bandage around my head. Precisely, by the bandage—I rationalized my predicament—and not by my almost complete blindness. However, when at times I tried to admit to myself that the problem was not at all caused by the bandage, that all that was left to me was but perception of smells and sounds—that never again would I perceive light and colour—I just couldn't stand it.

Any kind of grief is liable to become dulled eventually, and one can become accustomed to even the most terrible reality. Yet I showed no signs of ceasing to act oblivious to everything that happened around me. I responded absent-mindedly to the kindly but reproachful demands of our ward nurse Zoya; I ate my meals, went for treatment, and took strolls, supported by Masha Ivanova who accompanied me everywhere. I talked and sometimes even smiled.

However, twice a day, when the entire "sanatorium" gathered around the black dishes of the loudspeakers, I temporarily regained the sense of being part of a single whole, a soldier, and a daughter of a people whose territory had been invaded. And when the mournful and angry voice of Moscow brought the successive war communiqué to us, my individual plight dissolved in the common misery, as it were.

And then came 4 July, the day on which the heroic defence of Sevastopol came to an end. On that day, I suddenly became impatient of the hospital regimen; anxious to find out the truth about my eyesight, on my own initiative I took off the bandage. After a sharp flash of bright light and an acute attack of nerves, I temporarily became totally blind. This was an unexpected development both to myself and the hospital's opthalmologist, a middle-aged, thickset captain.

In the opinion of this medical officer, "the right eyeball wound caused by the penetration of a shell splinter" was quite serious, but should not have substantially affected the vision in my left eye. The treatment had proceeded normally—not too fast and not too slow—just as was usual in such cases. If only the bandage was removed some other time, on another day, perhaps everything would have turned out all right.

The medical officer has cautioned me that the most optimistic prognosis I could expect would be zero vision in my right eye and a partial vision recovery in the left one. One week, two weeks, three weeks... five weeks passed. I received treatment, including injections; the nurse changed my dressings and put drops in my eyes. Then my bandage began to be taken off in the doctor's semi-dark consulting room—for five minutes, then ten, and then twenty. Finally, the hospital front door flew open for me, and I was given permission to go out by myself.

It was my first opportunity to explore Sochi and it turned out to be truly beautiful. There were streets buried in foliage, palms, and the main attraction—the sea. The sound of its even, peaceful "breathing," as it were, came from a distance, port tugboats gravely called one another, and a fresh wind smelling of wide expanses pleasantly cooled my flashed face. The palms with their hairy trunks, looking as if they were bundled up in bearskins, formed up in a single line along the asphalt, right up to the turn in the road.

Suddenly, the tree at the end began to jump up and down, like a walking human being. It really was a human being, a lean old man wearing a wide-brimmed felt hat and supporting himself lightly on a long, crooked staff. As he walked past me, he undoubtedly noticed that I was nervous and behaved strangely, staring at him so. Very likely, the old man said to himself: "Apparently, she had never met a real shepherd; when she noticed me, she stood stock-still like a pillar of salt, as if confronted by an evil spirit...."

So the kindly Abhazian unwittingly became a harbinger of a great misfortune for me. A former machine gunner (that had been capable of bringing down accurate fire on enemy extended lines formed up half a kilometre away), I did confuse a human being with a tree! So it was not by accident that the distant space ahead of me was covered with iridescent mother-of-pearl, as it were. So it was not a mist but a terrible impairment of vision!

In the hospital wards and corridors, where space was limited by four walls, I was not as acutely conscious of my impairment. Stepping carefully, I walked along the sidewalk to measure the distance between the palms. The people who walked briskly on the other side of the road made a ridiculous clicking sound with the durable wooden soles of their sandals that civilians wore during the second summer of the war. Though I heard their footsteps, the pedestrians themselves were faceless to me. All I saw were the outlines of their heads and shoulders.

As I approached the corner of a house with the street sign attached to it, I decided I just had to know the name of the street, on which the hospital happened to be located. The even line of the white letters contrasting with the dark-blue background of the street sign was swaying; then it became blurred and trembled. I bit my lip until it bled and turned back.... "No, I must avoid taking strolls such as this," I cautioned myself mentally.

Then, by tripping me cunningly, the iron-plated rainwater gutter abruptly removed the sidewalk from under my feet, and threw me onto the soft asphalt, burning hot from the heat of the sun. I didn't hurt myself that much. My injuries were insignificant: a bruised knee and a scratched elbow. But the betrayal of the sidewalk, until recently so reliable and stable, was deadly....

And again the boring days in the hospital dragged on endlessly. The ward emptied more and more, my new acquaintances kept leaving Sochi one after another, and only Masha, dearest Masha remained to keep me company. Neither she nor I had any inkling of the fact that the senior medical staff of the hospital— who strongly believed that psychotherapy was more effective than the most potent medications—had been breaking the strict patient discharge regulations, for the director allowed Ivanova to remain in the hospital until I was discharged, in accordance with the wishes of my ophthalmologist.

Every day after supper, when the heat abated, Masha and I walked along the avenues running through the gardens surrounding the hospital.

One day, we were strolling along a narrow path toward the main building. As we approached a bench almost hidden under the heavy, lacquered leaves of the noble laurel, a short, thickset man, with an arm in a heavy cast, got up to give us his seat. Clad in officer's silk pyjamas, he held a thick cigarette in his mouth. It was Masha who noted all these details in the dark shadow and she instantly recognized the officer as he walked toward us. It was Colonel Neustroyev, Chief of Staff of our division.

"Comrade Colonel! Allow me...." Suddenly, forsaking the strict formality of address spelled out in Field Service Regulations, she ended completely informally: "So you're here, too, Parfentiy Grigor'yevich...."

"But I thought that nobody will recognize me in this attire," said Neustroyev, smiling sadly. "Where are you from, girls? Excuse me, I don't seem to remember you...."

Normally, rank and file don't associate with officers at the divisional level. However, everybody in our division knew Colonel Neustroyev. Thorough, sedate, and so amazingly simple and kind, he appeared to have no time to sleep. He had the tendency to arrive unexpectedly in the dispositions of his regiments. If an event in a regiment or battalion was worth sharing with other units, then Neustroyev would find time to pay them a visit, no matter how busy he might be; he would come even if he had to crawl to do it.

A few months earlier, it was Parfentiy Grigor'yevich Neustroyev who, together with Fink, chief of our Divisional Political Section, presented a Certificate of Merit to me on behalf of our army's Military Council. He then spent a long time in our permanent strong point describing the contemporary exploits of Nina Onilova. So our Divisional Chief of Staff did finally recognize us, though we, too, looked very different in our hospital attire.

When soldiers who had served in the same unit meet in a hospital, these encounters usually are quite predictable, regardless of the soldiers' age, personality, and habits. At first, they tend to exchange a few words about their wounds hastily and somewhat carelessly, as if discussing them was not important. Then—becoming artificially animated—they ask unrelated, muddled questions. Finally, almost instinctively they try to transform the conversation into a harmless, safe discussion of various past funny incidents and amusing queer things which happen in every unit in both quiet times and during heavy fighting, and which always become the property of the entire personnel.

However, a soldier such as myself, who happened to be flung onto a hospital bed in an earlier stage of a campaign, will sooner or later ask a most difficult question: "And what did really happen afterwards?" In a conversation such as this there are no seniors or juniors in rank.

Neustroyev's wound was painful and healed slowly, but was neither dangerous nor incapacitating. So, even though the Colonel had been evacuated from Sevastopol to the coastline of the Caucasus a few days before the city surrendered, he continued to be active and kept in touch with those who defended the stronghold until it capitulated.

Under the machine gun bursts fired by Messerschmitts, they put out to sea on inner tubes of tires, gasoline drums tied together, and partly smashed skiffs and hopper barges, and were saved both by a miracle, as it were, and by seamen's reckless bravery. It was from them that the command element of the Maritime Army learned how the defenders of the Khersones Lighthouse[6] kept their oath: "We'll stand to the last man!"

Parfentiy Grigor'yevich had never been verbose, no matter what he talked about, which was characteristic of staff officers. So he was used to sustaining even the most heart-to-heart talks with precise, brief remarks. However, there was no need for him to provide colourful details to those who had come to know the true value of the last piece of dried bread and the last cartridge clip—those who had lain behind their machine guns on Khersones rocks drenched with blood and sweat, dozing off briefly in the dead, chemical light of flares, and being startled by the heart-rending siren howl of enemy dive bombers. Names, surnames, dates—this was more than enough to generate in our minds an image of the recent past, with all of its grandeur and sorrow.

In the evening of the day we ran into Neustroyev, I went out onto the balcony. As I sat there, thinking, a southern night descended on the city, with its rising and falling crackle of cicadas, the rustle of leaves, and sighs of that kindly giant, the sea. Time passed swiftly. Masha had been asleep for a long time when I heard the gravel rustling under the feet of some reckless violators of our hospital routine, rushing home to catch at least an hour of sleep before daybreak. I was still sitting on the balcony, leaning against the warm stone railing and shielding my semi-blind eyes with one hand, when the motor of the water pump began to operate, as the water was being pumped into large saucepans in the kitchen.

So that's what happened. So they kept fighting even after all their ammunition had been exhausted; bandaged and with improvised splints, they attacked with bayonets. So they threw themselves under the tracks of armoured personnel carriers with their last hand grenade. So all of them had stayed behind, there, by the ruins of Khersones Lighthouse scarred by shrapnel — both those who were quite young and those who had gone grey long ago (including Major Shestopalov, commanding officer of our regiment, my platoon commander Morozov, and Kutsenko, about whom Masha and I inquired in every hospital in Sochi).

After all, it was they who made it possible for Masha, Samusev, Kozhevnikov, Sizov, and hundreds of other soldiers, to be evacuated. And it was they, too, who made it possible for me to sit here, on this balcony, already so much better, almost recovered, with impaired vision but nevertheless alive. Some of them dressed our wounds, others carried us to the lifeboats, and still others defended us stubbornly. Among the last were those who put of out action the detachment of an enemy gun aimed at our launch, and kept chasing away enemy dive bombers that were pursuing our defenceless little ship.

How was I to repay them? There was a way. The next day was to be my final medical examination. I knew I would not be permitted to return to the battle zone, and it would take several months before vision in my left eye would be restored. After all, one could study during these months. After all, there were other military specialties in addition to that of a machine gunner. Besides, no doubt, there were one-eyed hunters. So I would become one such hunter, too!

When our smart and stern ward nurse Zoya came to my room the next morning, she just couldn't hide her amazement. I was considered one of the most difficult patients in the ward. Anti-social and rude, I suffered from insomnia and refused to get up in the morning. However, this time I received Zoya with a smile. "What's for breakfast, my dear Zoya?" I asked cheerfully.

The nurse almost dropped her glass with thermometers. "Probably, 'shrapnel' with cucumbers, again," she said.

"Well, after all, 'shrapnel' is a type of porridge, too," I continued. "Pearl barley porridge is very good for you. Don't be surprised, my namesake. We simply smartened up last night. We had been thinking a lot; so we realized it's time to stop feeling sorry for ourselves. From now on we are bound to make steady progress."

In fact, from that day on both my mental and physical health began to improve rapidly. Two weeks after the final examination, I was ordered to appear in the hospital office. This meant that my treatment was coming to an end. The certificate given to me by a hospital clerk stated: "Fit to serve as a non-combatant in the rear." The postscript beside the big, round stamp at the bottom read: "Granted ten-day leave." However, I had no intention to return to the rear or go on leave.

I located Parfentiy Grigor'yevich Neustroyev and asked him to do me a personal favour and assist me in obtaining an assignment to a school for junior officers. So the Colonel, who remembered me as a capable machine gunner but knew nothing about the state of my vision, was glad to give me a note addressed to the chief of a forwarding point, in which he recommended that Sergeant Medvedeva be enrolled in a course for machine-gun platoon commanders.

Then came my final day and my final dinner at the hospital. Generous helpings of borscht with meat appeared on seven tables, covered with very clean tablecloths—straight from the laundry—and adorned with luxuriant bouquets of flowers. Altogether twenty-eight soldiers were leaving our "Voronezh Sanatorium" that day. We entered the dining room and sat down at the tables. And our usual, everyday, not so new uniforms instantly separated us from the rest of the hospital patients and staff, wearing grey flannel and white smocks respectively. Our uniforms broke up, as it were, all of our recently formed friendships with those staying behind in the hospital, no matter how strong and sincere they might have been at one time. From then on, to us— discharged patients—all those who donned uniforms on the same day as we did would become dearer, and more important and interesting.

After finishing eating, we silently filed out into the yard. The smokers rolled cigarettes—as thick and long as they could—in order to prolong the pleasure. They smoked greedily until they were satisfied, right up to the final, finger-burning draw.

"Fall In!" yelled Senior Lieutenant Samusev. As the most senior person in rank amongst us, he had the authority to check our names against his list. Then, as Samusev inspected the ranks with an officer's picky look, he reprimanded Ivanova, whom only that morning he had addressed simply as "dear Masha." Afterwards, having lifted a finger in a dashing gesture, he checked whether the little star of his field service cap worn on one side was located exactly above the bridge of his nose.

"Left Turn! Pace Setter, Quick March!"

The incredibly luminous Sochi summer, unruly in its generosity, brightened the sky, the land, and the sea. The bodies of two half-naked little boys, running beside our column, were dark like chocolate. The lucky little boys! They did not know what a tarpaulin boot with a rubber sole was like; they could run barefooted and splash in the sea. And then two young girls, walking under one particoloured umbrella, rushed toward us, both blond and wearing light flowered dresses.

However, I couldn't really see them properly. My impaired eye, affected by the bright sun, already ceased to distinguish details and was watering. With a furtive gesture, so as not to attract attention, I knocked off the tears. So be it! One could march in a column, even if blinded. I was determined not to be put out of action. Unless something happened that was beyond my control....

At the bus depot, Samusev checked the schedules and talked to the duty man and a middle-aged sergeant-major wearing overalls spotted with solar oil. Then he called us, Masha and me, aside.

"You can see for yourselves how big the crowd is. There is enough of our men to fill a bus. They will be taken right up to the forwarding point by a three-axle truck, which will leave from here with fuel, so the men can sit on the drums. As for you, take a brief rest, and in half an hour the duty man will put you on a bus; I've already got him to agree to do this."

We sat down on a bench, in a shadow of tall poplars. Even though the sun shone through their thick foliage, it was unbearably hot and burnt our faces; the sticky heat penetrated underneath our field shirts. Across from us a never-ending queue stood beside a wagon with aerated water, sold by a woman vendor. We heard the gay sound of glasses clanking and water splashing.

"No doubt, there is syrup to go with the water," I said quietly.

"Yes," Masha confirmed just as quietly, took some air through the nose, and added wistfully: "Cherry syrup. Only we haven't even got a penny."

In order to take my mind off our predicament, I began to search in my empty pockets. I shook out some crumbs, from a cake eaten long time ago, onto the palm of my right hand; and then I began to throw them onto the asphalt, tempting pigeons who were strolling on the square. A bold rock pigeon, with a sparrow's energy, fluttered over to the bench, and stealing up sideways right up to my legs, began to peck at the crumbs which had stayed in the folds of the thick tarpaulin of my boots.

The shadow which unexpectedly fell on the bird had frightened it. Madly beating its wings, the rock pigeon went up with a creaking sound, spinning, and almost knocked out two glasses filled with bubbling, apparently ice-cold aerated water, from the hands of an elderly woman who had approached the bench noiselessly.

"Thank you. You shouldn't have done it," I tried to protest, but the vendor refused to listen. She gave us each a glass and quickly returned to her wagon, beside which another line-up had already formed.

Then a rough voice announced that our bus was ready for boarding.

The chief of the forwarding point, who was a major of the Border Troops, decided our fate in a simple and fair manner. After reading

Neustroyev's note, he asked us a few questions regarding the design and operation of machine guns. Satisfied, he then reached for some papers.

"Were you together at Sevastopol? And in the hospital, too?" he asked. "Well, you may just as well continue serving together. We'll send you both to the Yeysk Machine-Gun School. This order will enable you to reach the School," he told us. However, the events unfolded not at all as the major expected them to unfold. He was as yet unaware that the strategic offensive of the German Army Group "South" had already began in the Rostov-Krasnodar sector.

CHAPTER IV

BREAKING OUT OF ENCIRCLEMENT

I tried to keep up with the rest. We approached the grove closer and closer by unequal, feverish jumps—with a heavy tramp of boots, hoarse, uneven breathing of people who were unaccustomed to running, and the abrupt whine of bullets which kept falling somewhere behind us. The Nazi tank gunner who fired at us with a machine gun was apparently inexperienced; the depression which lay in the path of the bullets distorted the distance and the frantic, long bursts all fell short of their aim.

Fleeing the Germans, we ran without firing a single shot. However, those who managed, during these frantic moments, to take a good look at Senior Lieutenant Samusev, who was advancing uphill by long bounds, were struck by the expression on his face of bold and daring high spirits—almost a triumph—a behaviour generally inappropriate in situations of this kind. No doubt, for this reason Samusev tried to stay behind our extended line, even though the swift little fountains of dust, rising in the yellowed grass, spurred him on, and forced him to run as fast as he could.

There was a kind of logic in Samusev's strange sense of pride that contradicted and overcame humiliation and fear. Even now, during the strange moments of our flight—not a panic-induced flight but one planned beforehand—he still considered himself as our commander. (A commander, whose plans, calculations, and stratagems would turn out to be superior to those of the enemy.)

There, near Sevastopol, in most difficult situations, everything was simpler. He was always subordinated to someone, was always part of a fighting team, and didn't have to make all the decisions, even in the fiercest engagements. However, here, in the steppe adjacent to the Sea of Azov, which was interspersed with a loose network of forest shelter-belts, it was he and he alone who was responsible for everyone and everything.

Four hours earlier—on the day this chapter begins—our group had been split in two; to put it bluntly, we were scattered by enemy tanks and an airborne assault force swiftly moving toward the south-east. We couldn't resist them; only Samusev and Nechipurenko, a fighter pilot who was sent to the infantry after recovering from a wound, were armed. Each of them had a Nagant revolver with about ten bullets. Yet, no one except Samusev knew at the time that Nechipurenko was armed and had been a pilot. Besides, Masha and I would have found it difficult to distinguish him from the seventy or so soldiers of our detachment consisting of former patients discharged from several military hospitals.

In the morning of that same day, when the thunder-like echoes of the distant artillery duel suddenly shifted from north to east, and were coming from an area in the vicinity of Krasnodar, Nechipurenko, after a brief consultation, had been instructed by Samusev to form a vanguard with several soldiers and to advance ahead of our group. The rest were to continue marching—no longer along the road but a short distance from it. The road proved to be deserted, except for a few collective farm women, riding in wagonettes on some urgent business. In a hurry to get back to their Cossack hamlets and large villages, they told us that "the artillery cannonade was heard in the Sea of Azov country for several days already."

There was something puzzling, sinister, alarming, and abnormal about the absence of military units, traffic controllers, and checkpoints in this district adjacent to the front. After dispatching observers to the road, Samusev ordered us to take cover upon seeing the first signs of any military unit approaching us. Unluckily for us, we suddenly heard a cicada-like crackling of speeding motorcycles, when we were still more than 2 kilometres away from the next forest. No matter how we rushed to reach the thick green foliage intersecting with the dusty yellow road, the forward patrol of an enemy airborne assault force, who drove heavy, four-cylinder motorcycles, reached the forest edge ahead of us.

A signal flare—like a smoky question mark—was suspended over the forest, and the light machine guns set up on the motorcycles opened up. But the Nazis did not suspect that they had run into an unarmed detachment. They only saw how, under their machine gun bursts, the Russian "Ivans" rushed forward and to the sides, as if trying to carry out a pincer movement against them.

Then the second flare went up, followed by the third. The motorcyclists backed up, without ceasing to spit out lead. From beyond the shelterbelt, tank main guns opened up, cutting off the forest area adjacent to the road by a fiery shrapnel brush. But by this time Samusev's group reached the safety of the forest.

There is always something especially threatening about an invisible, concealed enemy that doesn't return fire. For quite a long time, the enemy assault landing force kept combing the thicket, composed of alycha, acacia, apricot, and plum trees, with dense machine-gun and submachine-gun fire. Paradoxically, this enabled us to escape. Now each group had to fend for itself.

To run into an enemy force here, at least 100 kilometres from Yeysk, meant that the Germans had broken through, and it would be senseless for us to proceed according to our original itinerary. In addition to the already mentioned Nagant revolver, we had one compass, an ample reserve of coarse tobacco, six packets of wheat concentrate, two half-kilogram cans of stewed beef, and two medical bags. Moreover, some of us had knives; and Senior Sergeant Volodya Zarya, our sniper of Sevastopol fame, carried a telescopic sight in its case, carefully wrapped up in a pair of winter flannelette footcloths.

Our supplies, arms, and equipment were meagre, but the most terrifying, the most worrisome was our lack of orientation. We were relatively safe; here in the shelterbelt it would have been difficult to find us without dogs. Also, we were not likely to die from hunger, since there were many ricks of harvested grain nearby; here and there corn and sunflowers still grew in the fields, and Cossack villages were all around. However, we didn't know where to go, and whether the enemy assault landing force were carrying a raid behind our lines or were the vanguard of an advancing army. The second alternative would have been more ominous, by far, for us.

The fact that the district was so deserted, that the cannonade was moving along a gigantic arc farther and farther away to the south, and German aircraft formations were flying from time to time in that direction at high altitudes—all this implied that we should go back. However, Samusev could not yet bring himself to do this. The notion that the Germans already did as they liked here, in the Caucasus, seemed too unbearable and unnatural to him, and he hadn't yet fully realized that he was no longer obliged to follow the itinerary indicated in his map case.

So Samusev decided to keep advancing. At least until he identified the detachment of enemy troops we had encountered. From that moment on, his determination to proceed in this manner, rather than acting in some other way, forced Samusev to overcome even his internal voice of common sense. Apparently, for the first time he felt he was completely in charge, come what may. The repeatedly sharpened sense of responsibility on the part of Samusev had awakened in him the farsighted, calculated cunning of a Ukrainian chieftain, which was so necessary for a detachment leader planning to conduct a "forest war."

Moving along the shelterbelt, in about three hours we reached a deep and wide ravine. On the other side were orchards, white clay-walled cottages, and long buildings housing the livestock of a collective farm. We went to ground at the edge of the forest, without betraying our presence in any way. Having pulled out his precious sight from the thick bundle, Zarya began to study the peaceful scene in front of us, square by square.

In fifteen minutes Zarya detected what we all feared; he saw the dark masses of two tanks, vaguely distinguishable through the wire of a camouflage net carelessly covered with straw. The tanks were camouflaged between two ricks. To one side, where the wattle-fence came right up to the dusty road, the sharp eyes of the sniper detected the parapet of an artillery emplacement and the thin barrels of two anti-aircraft guns. There was a narrow stream meandering at the bottom of a depression thickly overgrown with reeds; and a multitude of marshy hummocks stretched in all directions from the banks of the stream.

"So.... I understand. In fact, it makes a great deal of sense to me. Let's try it. Let's definitely try it," said Samusev quietly, as he lay beside Zarya, peering into the telescopic sight. "The risk is moderate," he concluded. "The distance from the shelterbelt to the farm is about 1½ kilometres and to the stream, about 300 metres. The tanks are not likely to attempt negotiating the marsh. Let's immediately cross the shelterbelt with half of our people, while the other half remains in the forest. Starting from this spot, we'll go down in an extended line obliquely, as if trying to come out onto the western edge. We'll not hide. On the contrary, I'll order the men to take off their field shirts; the undershirts will be noticed sooner. We'll stop beside the water and get dressed, looking as if we are in doubt as to what to do next, and then we'll return to the forest. If the troops in the village are friendly, they'll identify themselves, and if they are German then they'll see that their prey is escaping; they wouldn't be able to resist firing at us. Though the slopes of the ravine are steep, at least they are dry. We'll have to run for about 40-50 seconds. Besides, aimed fire at a distance of about 2 kilometres is not so terrible, either."

"All the same, perhaps we shouldn't identify ourselves at this time, Comrade Senior Lieutenant," wondered Zarya, remaining unconvinced. "We could cover 10 kilometres before it gets dark—the shelterbelt stretches all the way to the horizon, and perhaps by then we'll locate friendly troops, if they happen to be in the area."

"The risk is minimal," Samusev said with conviction. "The Germans are not likely to expend their ammunition needlessly. There is no doubt we'll get away. On the other hand, we'll clarify the situation immediately. We already covered about 15 kilometres from the crossroads where we had run into the motorcyclists."

After Samusev discussed the plan with his non-commissioned officers, a thickset, well-knit Siberian with a nice-sounding and funny surname—Pel'mennykh—added a small but important detail to the plan:

"As soon as we begin to move, we should strew about coarse tobacco. First we should grind it and then strew it about. Of course, I am not comparing a [village] sheep dog to a husky.... Nevertheless, we should never underestimate sheep dogs, either. We should be extremely wary of them too."

* * *

With a dry rustling sound, a shell flew seemingly just above our heads. It hit with the grinding noise of its report, which merged with the sound of its discharge. "What a powerful gun," I thought. "This means that the tank is very heavy, so they wouldn't push with it into the marsh." The rumble of another such "duet" followed, again breaking the silence, and a second dirty-yellow bush, as it were, appeared on the slope just in front of the forest edge, but the forest was already about to shelter us. The injuries we sustained were minor. A bullet scratched one man's side, and a shell splinter caused a minor flesh wound to another one's left hand. This was not too high a price to pay for clarifying our situation.

It is difficult to say how many kilometres we covered that day. At any rate, many. I was very tired and the fatigue affected my vision. By evening, I couldn't see anything. I wandered in the dark, holding onto the tarpaulin strap of Masha's medical bag, orientating myself by the sound of her light footsteps. I was conscious only of the sharp little hammers of the pulse thumping against the temples in my heavy head, which felt as if it were filled with buckshot.

Marching about 100 metres ahead of our column, Pel'mennykh stopped it by announcing that the shelterbelt ended at a ravine. From that direction came the sound of dogs' barking, together with a faint odour of smoke. By this time, I could hardly move. Exhausted, I lay down on the ground, without seeing the medical bag which Masha attempted to place under my head. I grabbed her hand and began to whisper feverishly: "Mashen'ka! Please don't say anything about me to anyone.... Not a single word, do you hear me? Should we be surprised by the Germans, it would be best for me to dispatch myself immediately. Ask Samusev to let me have his Nagant revolver."

"Are you out of your mind? How could you even contemplate such a thing? And do you realize that the Senior Lieutenant...." Masha stopped short when she heard Samusev speak in a calm, slightly hoarse tenor: "Who has mentioned my name? Perhaps one of our two beauties did? And my face is covered with bristles, like those of a goblin."

"Remember, don't mention my eyesight!" I managed to whisper to my friend. Straightening my back with difficulty, I sat down, ran fingers through my hair, and with artificial animation invited Samusev to sit down beside us. "Please sit down, Comrade Senior Lieutenant. May we address you informally? Do fill us in on our situation."

Samusev sat down. He rustled a newspaper, tore off a little piece, and rolled up a cigarette. The little wheel of his lighter scratched the flint, and I smelled the sharp, tickling odour of a home-grown Abkhazian tobacco.

"Aren't you afraid of giving us away?" I said, perversely trying very hard to direct the conversation into "visual" channels. And no doubt I would have betrayed myself if Samusev hadn't been so absent-minded. "After all, I am smoking under my raincoat," he replied indifferently. Unable to maintain the tone, he added cryptically and with a sigh: "As to our plans, they are like those of the Odessa fortune-teller who had been warning everyone to beware of the authorities, and then herself was arrested for swindling her customers.... I sent a reconnaissance group ahead. Pel'mennykh went along with them; I thought that as a hunter he would be able to look after them. They'll return, report to us, and we'll then decide what to do. I must tell you, girls, that I pin great hopes on you. You'll have to guide us until we obtain weapons. We'll buy you civilian dresses; I've money for this. You'll walk together from village outskirts to village outskirts, behaving like girlfriends. Our lads all have shaved heads, hospital-style; anyone will identify them. On the other hand, you could pass for Cossack women because of your Sochi suntan. Also, your hairstyles are relatively normal."

"How can we act as guides, and without weapons to boot? And do you know, Comrade Senior Lieutenant," Masha spoke up unexpectedly in a rude tone, exclaiming "Ouch!" when I pinched her. "Shut up, Masha; do shut up, my dear!" I told her, turning to Samusev. "Don't mind me interrupting her, Comrade Senior Lieutenant. It's an excellent idea. I'll try to pretend that I am blind.... And Masha will lead me. Will you do it, Mashen'ka?"

"Y-yes," Masha confirmed after a short pause, but couldn't help remarking sarcastically: "What a valiant force we'll make with our blind reconnaissance and unarmed troops. How long can we last?"

"That's enough!" exclaimed Samusev, springing to his feet. "Do you realize you can be punished for talking like this in a battle zone!"

"Well, of course, she doesn't," I intervened in a quiet voice. "She doesn't know what's permitted and what's forbidden. Our Masha is one of a kind, so she says what is on her mind. However, at least she doesn't panic under fire. Do sit down, Comrade Samusev."

"I haven't got the time; I must go. I'll remember this conversation." And he went away, dry branches crunching under his feet.

"Listen to me, you reckless psychopath!" Masha's voice shook, as she was trying to control her temper. "What kind of scout will you make? You can't see, you can't run, and you can't write down anything. You can't reconnoitre. Have you forgotten what it involves?" Then it was my turn to get mad: "That will do! Have you forgotten what Neustroyev told us? Have you? Well, as for me, I just can't forget how our troops defended the Khersones Lighthouse. So I am determined to go reconnoitring."

The night passed virtually uneventfully. It was only after midnight that several single pistol shots rang out in the direction of the Cossack village and several drunken voices intoned a mournful, unfamiliar melody. Around 3:00 a.m., when the pre-dawn clouds, looking like brown pancakes, appeared on the "frying pan" of the sky about to turn blue, our scouts returned. Pel'mennykh carried a large jug of milk on his back, carefully wrapped in a raincape so that it wouldn't be noticeable and attract a sentry's attention. His companion, a merry, smart lad who was a tradesman and a former homeless orphan, managed to swipe a sack with three loaves of German bread, dazzlingly white but tasteless and rubbery, from a German army wagon. They brought us bad news.

We learned that the main elements of German units, principally motorized, did in fact break through, unimpeded. Rushing toward our defensive line, they rolled it back—how far, we didn't know. Behind the motorized units, wagon trains, columns of heavy, three-axle trucks, and tankers continuously advanced along the road for two days, under the cover of armoured personnel carriers and tanks. Already German garrisons have been set up in neighbouring Cossack villages. Though rather small, these garrisons were very well armed with machine guns and mortars, and sometimes also had armoured fighting vehicles at their disposal.

The garrison in the nearby village was especially strong. There was a well-protected store, and SS-men set up a kind of jail in a horse stable and in the various departments of the collective farm. Parties of prisoners of war were driven there in the evening, so that the guards might spend the night in comfort. The escort as a rule included 15-20 soldiers armed with light machine guns. Yet the tank crews in the village happened to be there by accident; they came either to carry out repairs or to get something to eat, and had been drinking already three days in a row.

"And who was it that fired the shots after midnight?" asked Samusev, concerned.

"I can't say for sure," replied Pel'mennykh. "However, I think the officers were simply having fun. Otherwise, the patrols wouldn't have been calmly strolling during the shooting."

The "council of war" consisting of two sergeants (Zarya and Pel'mennykh) and one senior lieutenant quickly decided to retreat through the shelterbelts, from forest to forest. By day, assisted by Masha and me, they were to plan how far they were to advance by night. However, first of all they had to obtain weapons. After giving the matter some thought, they decided to set up an ambush at a convenient spot by the road, to capture a lone motorcyclist or attack an officer's car without a large escort. To this end, our Nagant revolver with its nine cartridges represented a formidable weapon in the hands of the sniper Volodya Zarya. Also, by picking off one motorized patrol we could capture two submachine guns, and even a light machine gun.

A few hours later, a group of soldiers set up an ambush beside the highway, about 3 kilometres from the village. However, we were in for a surprise. At first a motor vehicle column with a heavy load went by along the road, raising dust; it was escorted by nine motorcyclists. Then a multicoloured, angular armoured personnel carrier with a long snout sped by. Half an hour later, a messenger, short of breath from fast running, reported to Samusev in a halting voice: "I saw a group of prisoners of war being driven here. There are about fifty of them. All are bandaged and covered with blood. One of them apparently couldn't go on and squatted down, so he was shot immediately... on the spot...."

"How many guards are there?"

"About ten privates, one non-commissioned officer, and one mounted officer. They have a horse-driven cart, the driver of which is apparently unarmed."

"So that's that," recapitulated Samusev. "Back you go and keep your eyes open. Use the agreed signals. If you see any vehicles, make the sound of a raven, and if infantry, of the cuckoo bird."

"Yes, Sir!" replied the messenger.

"Well, what shall we do, Sergeants?" asked Samusev.

"We must rescue them. Apparently, there is a reason why the prisoners are being driven toward the front. We're convinced the Nazis must have some kind of dirty trick in mind."

Samusev warned the Sergeants: "Remember that if shots are fired we'll all be killed. The tanks can get here from the village in a mere 15 minutes. We've a chance to succeed though...."—here Zarya and Pel'mennykh held their breath—"provided we act quickly and resourcefully. We'll use sand, boots, and hands instead of weapons. We'll blind the enemy soldiers with sand; kick them in the stomach with boots; and choke them with our hands. We are bound to succeed, provided the Nazis don't recover their wits. Zarya, take half of the men and quickly cross the road. We'll jump them from both sides."

"Come on guys, let's give them a hard time!" Narrowing his eyes, Pel'mennykh pulled out his hunting knife from its sheath, to test the speed of the process. Bending toward the ground and walking silently in a manner of a taiga native, he dove into the bushes.

The forest deposited twenty men, unarmed but terrible in their fury, onto the road. Like a broken string of a musical instrument, Samusev's penetrating, ringing shout—"Battalion!"—shot up over the road. But there was no need for this boyish stratagem, for the prisoners reacted with lightning speed. The precise formation of the escorts, each of whom was grabbed by four, six, eight prisoners—grabbed bulldog-like, fighting to the death—immediately broke up into several balls, as it were, made up of entangled bodies rolling along the shoulders of the road.

Quick like a released spring, a prisoner wearing an officer's field shirt dashed toward the *Ober-Leutnant*. With both hands he tore into the officer's patent leather belt and jerked it forward. Falling over toward his right stirrup, the officer pulled out a heavy Walther from its holster. He stunned the prisoner by hitting him twice with the weapon, and raised his horse on two legs, but to no avail. A quiet click of a shot was heard and the horse began to fall to the ground clumsily.

The hammer of a Walther is self-cocking like in a revolver. The *Ober-Leutnant* did manage to pull the trigger three times in the last few seconds before he died. At any rate, this had no effect on the outcome of the skirmish. Not expecting anyone to come to the prisoners' rescue, and stunned by the bold and swift attack, the escorts couldn't offer serious resistance. None of them had the time to open fire and they were at a disadvantage in hand-to-hand fighting—the prisoners' yearning for freedom was so strong, as was the aspiration of Samusev's men to acquire weapons.

Then Zarya, who had drilled in hand-to-hand fighting with several marines in Sevastopol, reached by several bounds a German soldier whom he had selected beforehand. Afterwards he tore into the barrel of the Schmeisser raised by the German, pulled it toward himself and then to one side, and hit him in the abdomen with his knee forcefully. Without changing the position of the captured submachine gun, Zarya tackled yet another guard, who had attacked him, with a sharp blow to the bridge of the nose. He flung aside the instantly-blinded enemy soldier into the deadly embraces of some of the prisoners. After picking up a second enemy submachine gun, Zarya threw himself into the thick of the scuffle. Soon it was all over, and not a single Nazi survived. Meanwhile, the frightened team sped into the shelterbelt and stopped only when the trap became stuck in an impenetrable thicket.

Subsequently, the men began to "fraternize" on the road. Samusev's brief order: "Go into the forest, immediately! Clear the road! Don't leave even the slightest trace of the skirmish!" interrupted their bear-hugging and incoherent expressions of gratitude.

We gathered beside the trap, about one hundred paces from the crossroads. It took us a long time to count our booty. In addition to the weapons we had taken away from the guards, there were several boxes with ammunition for submachine guns in the trap, as well as a flare pistol, a cartridge pouch full of thick cartridges marked with multi-coloured paint, about thirty hand grenades, dry rations for the guards, and two containers with excellent drinking water.

Masha and I bustled about, caring for the wounded. The prisoner wearing an officer's field shirt turned out to be a battalion commissar; he and Samusev sat down under a branchy alycha tree. After briefly describing the situation in this sector of the front and relating the story of the prisoners who had been captured by German units that had penetrated into the breakthrough of the front, the battalion commissar lifted his eyes. "Does this mean that we'll be breaking out together, Comrade Commissar?" asked Samusev.

"I wish we could!" the commissar exclaimed, chasing away an insect about to sit down on his eyebrow, cut by the blow of the Walther. "There are so many wounded amongst us. We can't march quickly, so we'll try something else. The strongest among us will don German uniforms. The Nazis are self-disciplined, thank God. If they see an officer, they'll talk only to him. And I happen to be fluent in German; I worked for two years in a trading agency. So I'll act as a spokesman for the group. Of course, our twenty captured submachine guns would be most useful to us as well. Unfortunately, for the time being we must part. By the way, you should also take two or three German uniforms; they'll come in handy." He got up with difficulty and started to take off his field shirt.

An hour later, when the dust had settled and covered the reddish-brown blood stains, the "prisoners" were formed up again. Three of them —in the vanguard, centre, and rearguard of the column—carried submachine guns under their greatcoats and ragged raincapes. Beside the commissar, who had pulled on the uniform of the *Ober-Leutnant*, two expert hand grenade throwers perched themselves on the trap. Eight well-groomed "guards" again escorted the column of pitiful prisoners of war.

On parting, the battalion commissar embraced Samusev and slipped into his pocket a note which he had hastily composed. It read: "Your prospects for reaching our authorities are better. Don't take any foolish chances and use your head, so that you would be the one to outwit the Germans, and not vice versa. Moreover, remember I am leaving you the map case of an *Ober-Leutnant* of the Abwehr [Army Counterintelligence —Trans.] and its contents. Take good care of it."

"Well, friend, it's time to go." The commissar turned Samusev around sharply and propelled him forward gently. Then the column started to move.

In half an hour, we abandoned our bivouac as well. We had gained our first victory and had left behind the first casualties since our discharge from various hospitals. After marching for three hours, we stopped for a rest. It would have been dangerous to continue advancing, for the shelter-belt began to thin out. A village was situated nearby, and a distant, lazy sound of dog barking came from that direction. After considering our situation, Samusev led his group back into the woods and then he, Zarya, and Masha crawled up to the forest edge. Samusev decided not to take any chances, so he instructed Masha as follows: "Listen, Masha. Go back right away. Take two field shirts, cut the sleeves off, and improvise a skirt for yourself. Put it on along with a makeshift vest. Don't forget to cover your head with a kerchief. Grab a handful of brushwood. Meanwhile, we'll observe the village cabins."

After Masha crawled away, Samusev and Zarya hid in nearby bushes to observe a low, little adobe dwelling, resembling a shed, on the outskirts of the village. A deep sounding hum startled them. Samusev swore when he lifted his head. A heavy, furry bumble-bee with golden little lumps on its rear legs flew into a spider web, turned around in the sticky threads, extirpated itself with difficulty, and flew away. "What a daring, little tramp!" Zarya exclaimed with envy. "If only we could escape the way it did!"

"We are going to make it," Samusev replied confidently. "The Nazis have other things on their minds than what goes on behind their lines. They are rushing forward recklessly. There is no front, only marching formations. I am certain we'll bypass them in some places and in others we'll break through."

"Well, well...." Zarya plucked a furry sorrel leaf, and began to chew it, smacking his lips with pleasure. "Is it a good idea to send Masha to the village? Perhaps it would be better if I go?"

"She has braids," Samusev said gruffly. Then, realizing that Zarya did not know what he was talking about, explained: "Masha has kept her braids, while Zoya was given a boyish haircut; it would be too dangerous for her to go. Unlike Zoya, Masha can pass for a village woman. Though her boots are somewhat inappropriate, here, in the Kuban' territory, peasant women, too, wear boots. By the way, I trust your Schmeisser will not miss at a range of 100 metres."

"I can assure you it will not miss at 200 metres, either."

"Do you see that rick?" asked Samusev. "You're to go there to take up your firing position and cover Masha, before she comes out of the bushes. In turn, we'll cover you from here. Thus, our 'defence' will be disposed in 'echelons.' Everything will be done according to the rules."

After Samusev and Zarya had been observing the village for almost four hours, their minds were set at ease. During all this time, only once did a woman—apparently middle-aged and carrying a stick and a yoke —come out of the outermost adobe cabin. And when Masha, dressed in her home-made outfit and resembling a beggar or a mummer, was about to leave, a cart with a red-brown cow harnessed to it drove out of the yard of the cabin, advancing toward the shelterbelt through a stubble field.

"Instead of reconnoitring, we'll resort to civilian diplomacy," uttered Samusev, satisfied.

The woman, who was whipping her cow with a long stick, was younger than the one who had come out of the cabin to get water. Bending down from time to time, she kept gathering handfuls of golden straw from the stubble field and throwing them into the cart. Apparently, the village utilized as fuel the remains of the last grain crop which had been harvested hastily and somewhat carelessly, and possibly subsisted on it too. Closer to the village, the stubble field was clear and tidy. Here, too, beside the shelter-belt, still lay sheaves of unthreshed wheat, dry like powder.

The young woman was approaching the forest edge gradually. When she was situated about fifty paces from Samusev, he touched Masha's elbow lightly and said: "Now is the time." When she saw Masha emerging from behind the bushes, the Cossack woman stopped, alerted. However, after only a few moments she overcame her shyness, to be expected under the circumstances, and started to advance toward Masha. The two women engaged in a quiet discussion and then walked together in the direction of the forest edge.

The name of our new acquaintance was Varya. She told us that there were no Germans in her village. German scouts on motorcycles and armoured personnel carriers kept dropping in, as did tankmen, but did not stay long. "'Mother, give us eggs.... Mother, gives us milk....' they kept saying. They would stuff themselves with food, splash in the spring, and then drive away.... There is a lot of them in the villages close to the road, but we are out of the way, thank God. They shot all the village chickens and ducks they could lay their hands on.... Our women are cunning like cats and buried everything they could in the ground. But we'll give you both food and wine."

"Forget about wine; we need water! We've had only one cup per person all day," said Samusev.

"In a flash," promised Varya. "Only let me take the cart back and talk to my women neighbours. Will you come with me?" she turned to Masha. The latter gave Samusev a questioning look. He nodded in approval. "While you're in the village, ask for some clothing for yourself and Zoya. You make poor costumers. In your outfit you're liable to scare off any patrol," Samusev told Masha.

After entering the semi-dark and cool village home, Masha emptied a cup of thick, cold milk in one gulp and then, exhausted, lowered herself onto a wide bench. Meanwhile, Varya, bare-headed and rosy-cheeked, rushed about the kitchen, making a smacking sound with her bare feet on the adobe floor. Her mother, the middle-aged woman whom Samusev and Zarya had observed in the telescopic sight, went to consult the neighbours.

Almost all of the inhabitants of this tiny village were related by blood or marriage, so Varya's appeal apparently struck a responsive chord in her relatives. Yet kinship was likely not the only reason for their generosity: in less than three hours the cart was filled to overflowing. A tub full of water, covered with clean sacking, rose above the other contents of the cart. At the bottom lay two huge sailcloth bags with fresh home-made bread baked on cabbage leaves, and pieces of slightly salted lard, three to four fingers thick. There was butter in a good saucepan, clay pots filled with fruit dumplings with cream, pies, and eggs.

These provisions simply amounted to a treasure in the second year of the war, so Masha was beside herself with amazement. Had she been older and more experienced, she would undoubtedly have noticed how difficult it was for Varya's three children to keep their eyes off the food that was being piled up onto the cart. But Varya's and her neighbours' joy was so genuine that Masha had not the slightest inkling of the obvious— if the peasants had plenty of everything, why would they be picking untreshed ears of wheat?

Masha and Varya waited for the onset of darkness to start for the forest. Heavily leaning on her yoke, the cow paced slowly, brushing aside Varya's vigilant whip like insects. Having exchanged her home-made outfit for a grey, tightly-woven linen skirt, a roomy blouse, and a kerchief with a polka dot design, Masha looked like a real village girl. Under the straw, concealing—just in case—the precious cargo, a set of women's clothing intended for me was hidden as well.

As the cart squeaked rhythmically, a flock of sparrows flew past with a rustling sound in the still evening air, and quails whistled their own thing while feeding in the stubble field. Only the distant thunder of the artillery cannonade, rolling away more and more to the south—a sound which could not be heard in daytime and was barely audible then, in the silence of the twilight—reminded you that war was going on.

It was completely dark by the time Varya and Masha reached the shelterbelt. The soldier who had replaced Zarya at the advanced listening post took a good look at the women's faces and silently stepped forward, grabbing one horn of the cow with his free hand. Solely on the basis of the irritability with which he was pulling the tired cow, Masha realized how thirsty were the men waiting in the thicket for the arrival of the heavy tub filled with water.

Our soldiers drank their fill until they almost choked, using objects at hand, such as mess tins, lids and German helmets, picked up at the site of the skirmish. They would have drank the entire tub of water had not Samusev come to his senses and shouted that they must save some for later.

Then they sat down in groups to eat, both satisfying their hunger and laying in store for the future. It made no sense for us to take the pots and utensils, so we decided to leave them behind. On the other hand, we designated bread and lard as "emergency rations." Finally, Samusev glanced at his watch; it was close to eleven. So he called Zarya, instructing him to observe the south-eastern sector of the sky as attentively as possible. Then he accompanied Varya, who was in a hurry to return home, to the forest edge, since he wanted to ask her for detailed directions.

On reaching the forest edge, they stopped. Samusev opened his map case and took out a wad of bills. Extending them to Varya, he said: "Here, take it."

"Are you crazy; the neighbours will scratch my eyes out, should they find out," she protested. "The Germans play the master here; they make themselves very much at home, and I am to take money from my own people! After all, this was a joint gift."

"Please take the cash. You've three children; it'll come in handy...."

"The children have a mother. Also, the collective farm has fed us in the past and it'll look after us until the war ends. No. Put it away. Put it away, or I'll get mad. Listen, Senior Lieutenant." New, unfamiliar notes sounded in Varya's voice. "On your way back, as you're chasing the fleeing Germans, do stop at our village for a drink...." Suddenly she raised her arms, pulled the embarrassed Samusev toward her, kissed him on his cracked lips, and immediately pushed him away. "Keep well... merchant." Then Varya went away quickly, whipping the heavily breathing cow.

Samusev stood motionless for a few minutes and then turned back. It was well into the night, and there was still a great deal to do before daybreak. As soon as he returned to our camp, Zarya reported to him: "At 2330, two flares, one green and one red, were observed in the indicated sector, at an interval of 10 seconds."

"Did the green one appear first?"

"Yes, Sir!"

"And what was the distance?"

"Difficult to say, Comrade Lieutenant. At any rate, considerable. Close to the limits of visibility. I've almost missed the first flare."

"This means that the battalion commissar and his men have gone a long way. Well done!" Samusev hesitated for an instant. "Well, all right. Let's go."

And again we walked until dawn; we advanced at a speeded up pace, this time with our arms at the ready. The flares released by the commissar's group meant that the main stream of German columns was moving parallel to the road and, if it deviated, it did so toward the south. Therefore, Samusev led us in a more northerly direction, to cut across the path of the enemy assault landing force; he believed that it would be easier to cross the front lines on the flank of the advancing Nazi units. To the right, nearer to the road, marched a patrol commanded by Zarya, consisting of six soldiers armed with submachine guns and hand grenades. Three extra armed men made up the advanced guard, a supply "train," and a "medical unit." By the way, Masha and I had only two first-aid packets each left in our medical bags. But we no longer felt like troops that were encircled. We considered ourselves an infantry detachment advancing in our own, albeit temporarily occupied land.

The next day we rested in the open, in the steppe; we found ourselves quite a distance from the shelterbelt we had already passed and 10 kilometres from the one ahead of us. By the distant roar of engines, we became aware of the approach of yet another motor vehicle column. Strictly speaking, the movement on the road continued throughout the night and the Nazis kept to their main routes. From time to time, some reckless road hog lit up the darkness with the bright beams of his untinted headlights, without observing the dimout, but this did not affect us.

It was quite different in daytime. Probably, the visibility from the high bodies of the huge three-axle German trucks was extensive, and Samusev avoided taking unnecessary risks. About 1-1½ kilometres from the road, in a shallow hollow sloping toward the north, we found a flimsy, half-ruined shed. The spring that was gushing out slightly to the side of the shed kept filling a shallow stream with icy water, pure like dew. Even now, in August, a luxurious juicy grass grew all around. In the shadow of the spreading willows, there were stakes driven firmly into the ground; perhaps these were vestiges of benches or the common table of a field work team. No doubt, a field camp had been located here at one time.

It was here that our team—the "Sevastopol Battalion" (as we began to call ourselves in earnest the previous day)—stopped for a day's rest. Four soldiers armed with submachine guns went on patrol. The others, yearning for running, unrationed water, almost drank the stream dry. For the first time in two days we washed ourselves properly. Then the soldiers blissfully stretched on heaps of rotting straw and old rags, and began to snore discordantly.

Only two soldiers—Masha and I—could not count on resting at this long-awaited halt. We were charged with a reconnaissance mission, to find out what awaited the "Sevastopol Battalion" on the other side of the next shelterbelt, a dark fringe that bordered the shining blue sky along the horizon. Samusev did realize that after marching for two days it would be very hard on us, two young girls, to cover another 30 kilometres (in daytime we had to go as far as the next suitable shelter and back, and at night we were to lead the troops there). However, our commander had no choice in the matter. Incidentally, the clothing obtained by Masha at Varya's village transformed Masha and me completely.

The instructions which Samusev gave us on seeing us off were very simple. "Don't go too far beyond the shelterbelt; about 5 to 7 kilometres, not more. You needn't take any weapons; that's not where your strength lies. You should note your reference points well, so that you'll not get lost at night. Should you run into some Nazis, keep calm. Just in case you're interrogated, you're from the village of Krinichnyy. You've heard that a large state farm had been disbanded in a village in the vicinity of Ver- khovskaya, and you want to buy some sheep from this farm. Here is your money." Squatting, Samusev took handfuls of black soil and began to rub it into the new bills thoroughly. "By the way, don't volunteer to show your money. Show it only when you are forced to do it. You should pretend that you're neither pro-Soviet nor anti-Soviet, but merely wish to take advantage of the big opportunity to buy a few sheep at a reduced price."

"What?!" I exclaimed involuntarily. "I would rather die than play that kind of a role...."

"You fool!" Samusev interrupted me rudely. For the first time, I sensed that he was truly angry. "We don't want you dead; all we want from you is intelligence. There is no need to play the part of Mary Stuart [Mary, Queen of Scots—Trans.]. If necessary, you'll even be called upon to fraternize with the Germans. As long as I am your superior you'll carry out my orders. Understood?"

"Comrade Senior Lieutenant! I didn't...."

"Never mind. We'll continue this conversation some other time. Get ready. You two will have the opportunity to discuss the mission I've assigned to you on the way. What's more," he said, already calming down, "try to return before twilight, so that you may have time for a brief rest at least, before we start moving."

* * *

It was a bright August morning as we strode over soft grass, covered with dew, trying to select the best possible route and remember it as best as we could. On the way, we noted a cool, steep-sided bolder, a clump of unruly hazelnut bushes, a broken up horse-cart apparently abandoned the previous autumn—and a rick of semi-rotted hay.

Masha marked out the route and I, like a schoolgirl, mentally repeated the reference points, moving my lips (during the "blind" months at the hospital my memory became unusually sharp). Even though we each had a pencil and a package of cigarette paper, we decided not to make any notes, so as not to risk being betrayed by them in the event we were searched.

Close to the next shelterbelt, we came across the evidence of a recent engagement: black holes made by mine explosions, hastily dug foxholes, and piles of spent cartridge cases. We concluded that the fighting had taken place only one or two days earlier. As we approached the forest holding hands and trying to stay calm, we saw along the edge black soil dug up with tank tracks and tear-like drops of resin that shone on trees mutilated by machine-gun bursts. An acrid smell of burning was coming our way. After some hesitation, we entered the undergrowth, moving away the moist foliage with our hands and making our way through the forest.

Here, in unstable waves, acrid fumes floated in the oblique sun rays that had penetrated the thicket. Giving way softly, the thick carpet of fallen leaves dampened the sound of our footsteps. From time to time, birds burst into a song, friendly as at daybreak. I listened to them—there was no alarming chatter of a magpie in this birds' choir, meaning that there were no people nearby.

About thirty paces beyond the forest edge—thick and flattened, as it were—the steppe opened in front of us again, or rather not the steppe but a cultivated field, strictly speaking. It was a stubble field, covered with ungathered ricks, which stretched all the way to the horizon. We took a look all around without emerging from the bushes.

Some 3 kilometres to the left, the shelterbelt proceeded toward the north sharply, almost at a right angle. The area seemed entirely deserted. To the right, also at a distance, obviously near the highway, something showed black by the forest edge. Directly ahead of us, along our route and apparently at the same distance, we detected what seemed a small, round grove.

After consulting one another, we decided to go as far as the grove and then return. But when we covered half of the way, we realized we had been mistaken about the grove. It turned out to be a single tree— a tall, thick giant of a willow spreading its powerful branches over the field —so wide that at a distance it appeared to be a group of trees. It would have been foolish on our part not to take advantage of such an ideal observation tower.

But the task proved to be far from easy. When Masha tried to reach the lowest branch by a running jump, she just couldn't do it. We even gathered all the rocks in the vicinity to make a kind of "trampoline," but to no avail. Then I climbed onto this shaky pyramid and went down on my knees facing the grey-brown, cracked bark.

"Climb onto my shoulders," I ordered her.

Masha obeyed me. I grabbed the trunk of the willow and drew myself to my full height. At once I felt my temples throb intensively and rainbow-coloured rings began to dance before my good eye.

"Can you reach it?" I asked Masha.

"No, Zoya, it's just a bit short."

"Then climb onto my head."

"What about you? What about your wound?"

"Damn! Do hurry it up or else I am bound to fall down. Hurry!" I urged her. Pushing off from her live support, Masha finally managed to grab a thick, bumpy branch with both hands. Scratching and scraping the trunk with her bare feet, she raised herself and instantly disappeared into the foliage. I immediately moved away from the willow, staggering, and lay down with both hands over my face, trying to breathe deeply and evenly. The pain, which was squeezing my head like a hoop, went away slowly. Then the grey foam in front of my eyes became lighter and began to dissolve.

At least half an hour went by, but there was no sign of Masha. I raised myself to a sitting position and carefully examined the crown of the tree; Masha's grey skirt was nowhere to be seen. "Masha, are you there? Are you lost?" I shouted.

"They should be lost, the 'pagan' Nazis, I mean.... Trucks keep moving along the road; I counted eighty-seven of them — all going south. And here..." she hesitated. A barely audible, deep-sounding roar originated and floated in the air, as it were. "And here are the tanks.... Ten.... Another ten.... Still more of them.... Look, look! Listen, Zoya. There is a tank by the shelterbelt as well. And I see a smoke rising, perhaps from a campfire. It wouldn't be wise to advance in a straight line here. We should swerve to the right, at an angle to the shelterbelt. Well, I am coming down; I've seen enough."

In a few minutes, turning sharply to the north, we again strode across the field. Suddenly, a tall man, wearing a German, toad-like split raincape, stepped out from behind a high, last-year's stack, and walked toward us. He threw aside a flap of his cape; a ribbed pistol butt was protruding from the pocket of his dirty blue riding breeches. "Well! Come here! Let's get acquainted!" he shouted.

We couldn't run. At such a distance it would have been impossible for him to miss should he fire at us. Angry and ashamed, we approached the stranger slowly, sensing how clumsy, bulky, and altogether too visible our bodies had become. The tow-haired lad, his unshaven face covered with bristles, appeared calm and confident. "Did you look for eggs in crows' nests? This is fall; you won't even find empty shells in them."

I instantly switched to the local Russian-Ukrainian dialect, explaining that we were looking for a missing chestnut calf with a white patch on his head. "The accursed calf has been missing for three days; I fear that some soldiers might have put him in a cauldron...."

"Wait, wait," the tow-haired man interrupted me, leaning forward with his entire body as he peered into my face. "So that's it. You've adjusted to the new situation very quickly.... Where is your uniform, Sergeant?"

"What uniform?" Frozen with fear, I nevertheless tried to maintain my previous tone.

"Stop playing the fool! You were hospitalized. In Sochi. Both of you. I don't remember you," he turned to Masha, pointing at her with a dirty finger, "but I saw her in the 'Voronezh Sanatorium.' The day before yesterday, an assault landing force had scattered you with machine guns near Yeysk. And now you're here. Perhaps your group is not too far away, either. Lead me to them. After all, I was a member of your group. Or are you hiding under someone's skirt?"

I was thinking feverishly. "Was this man from our detachment? I've never seen him. Maybe I didn't recognize him because of my impairment. Why then hadn't he noticed Masha? He knew about us, so he must have been in Sochi, but whence the German uniform? Did he switch sides; was he hired by the Germans as a policeman? In that case, he ought to have immediately arrested us. Perhaps he wants to spy on us, in order to get through to our troops? What are we to do now?"

The tow-haired man was apparently fed up with us. "Why aren't you giving me an answer? Well, you don't have to." He pulled out his left arm from under the cape; in his fingers he tightly held a hand-rolled cigarette. After flicking his lighter, he released a cloud of acrid smoke from his mouth. "I don't care. Take a walk. Look for your calf. In the meantime I'll take it easy." Without looking around, he dropped to the ground, leaned his thickset, broad body against the stack, and spread out his short legs, clad in boots that had turned a reddish colour. "Well, go

—what are you waiting for! The calf could indeed end up in a cauldron!" he added, impatiently. Then he demonstratively turned away, and began to whistle: "A lad took a stroll at sunset... [a popular song]."

Feeling doomed, we started walking slowly, and kept looking around every minute or so. We didn't know what to do. Should we go back to our day camp and unwittingly betray our troops? Should we return to the little village on this side of the shelterbelt? Suppose German troops are stationed there; didn't the tow-haired one himself come from that direction? Should we wait here?

None of the alternatives made any sense. However, an instinct prompted us to continue moving in the previous direction, but without showing that the unexpected encounter had ruined our plans. By the way, by approaching the boundary between the two shelterbelts, we gave the impression that our destination was the nearby village.

"Masha, keep an eye on him, at least, and don't lose him," I asked her after covering about fifty paces.

"He is sitting down and having a smoke, as if he didn't care at all about us. What a pig!" she retorted, disgusted.

"Well, let's keep walking. Maybe we'll come up with something," I offered.

Oh, how difficult it was to walk under the hot sun along the rough, prickly stubble field, knowing that any step we might take in any direction could turn into an irremediable mistake. Suppose we take a step, and suddenly a pistol shot clicks behind our backs. Suppose we take a step, and at that moment the tow-haired one decides that he doesn't want his prey to escape too far, so he summons his comrades by whistling. They grab us and drag us away to be tortured and defiled. Suppose we take a step, and this very step—to one side of the shed sheltering our comrades—turns out to be our very last, and we are prevented from telling them what route they should follow.

Terrified, we kept walking—silently, in a straight line, and sensing with our stiffened backs the black "pupil" of the imaginary gun sight. We approached the shelterbelt as if in a trance, and hid in the undergrowth. Then Masha took a careful look from behind the bushes. "I see him walking—there he is!" she exclaimed squeezing my hand tightly. But I was unable to distinguish the figure in the camouflage raincape.

"Where is he going?"

"Back. Towards the willow."

Indeed, the stranger slowly walked away in the opposite direction.

Masha said that he made a running jump, apparently over a ditch, the one we had also crossed. By then we were both convinced the tow-haired one was not going to pursue us, after all; he didn't turn around even once. This reinforced our new belief that he was not an enemy. Perhaps he was a friend, after all? During the few hours we spent in the composite group, consisting of former patients of various hospitals, Masha might well have failed to memorize every face. However, if he were a friend, why did he react so calmly—almost indifferently—to our refusal to recognize him? Why didn't he demand it, insist on it, and shout at us?

Out of prudence, we stayed where we were for some time, observing the single wayfarer until he disappeared from view. And then we made our way through the bushes, emerging into the steppe. Afterwards, we ran as fast as we could.

Neither Masha nor I suspected that it was not the tow-haired man who, in the camouflage cape, went back toward the old willow. We didn't notice that the tow-haired man went behind the stack, after letting us cover sufficient distance; he then moved the sheaves apart and uttered a few words. Another man, also unshaven and dirty and armed with a short German carbine, emerged from the stack with difficulty. The two men consulted one another briefly. Then the second man put on the camouflage raincape, came out into the open, and started walking toward the willow. On the other hand, the tow-haired one reached the ditch by crawling behind the stack, slid into it like a snake, and then walked toward the road.

As we were running across the steppe, having satisfied ourselves that the man wearing the cape had no intention to spy on us, a very well concealed observer was waiting for us at the forest edge. It was the tow-haired lad, and his keen eyes instantly focused on our two bright silhouettes and followed them.

The sun was setting when we—tired and out of breath—finally reached the shed. When Samusev saw how agitated and frightened we were, he understood that something unexpected had happened. "Reveille! Take up arms! You've five minutes to get ready," he ordered. Then, taking us to one side, he asked: "What's the matter? Speak up!"

However, before we had a chance to report, we heard a loud altercation through the wide open door. In a while appeared the sentry, his submachine gun inconsiderately urging our tow-haired stranger. When the latter was pushed into the shed, Samusev immediately let out a cry of joy: "Nechipur! You flying devil!"

Next they were stamping in one spot, bear-hugging each other and scattering the rags that covered the earthen floor. The soldiers standing in a tight circle around them expressed their amazement by exclamations of joy. However, Masha and I hid in a corner, terribly ashamed of our double slip-up: we didn't recognize a friend and failed to notice that we were being tailed. We were so embarrassed we didn't dare to look into each other's eyes.

The bearded, tow-haired lad turned out to be Georgiy Nechipurenko, a former fighter pilot who was transferred to the infantry after he had been wounded (as had been mentioned above). Though he had no previous experience in fighting on the ground, he was to become quite a good soldier.

Following Samusev's order, Nechipurenko's vanguard had orientated themselves by his pilot's map of the North Caucasus. Because he led his men in a straight line, by morning of the first day Nechipurenko managed to outdistance Samusev's "Sevastopol Battalion" by some 25 kilometres. Advancing slightly at an angle to our route, Nechipurenko's men reached, before Masha and I did, the shelterbelt area where a few days earlier an advanced guard of a German airborne force had fought with a Soviet reserve company.

Apparently the fighting had been prolonged and fierce. The soldiers of the company defending the forest edge had several machine guns and anti-tank rifles, and offered desperate resistance. The Russians burnt down one enemy armoured personnel carrier, knocked out one tank which had broken through toward them from the rear, and killed quite a few of the German troops, but were themselves almost all wiped out too. Nechipurenko's men, having combed the shelterbelt, picked up several weapons missed by the German "booty men": five trilinear rifles, one Simonov semi-automatic weapon with a flat dagger-like bayonet, and a German carbine.

Nevertheless, the firepower of these weapons was insignificant. Only the carbine magazine was full, while the ammunition for the Russian rifles had been completely exhausted. Nechipurenko's men also discovered a machine-gun nest, smashed by a direct hit. In the breech casing of the maimed Maxim, a piece of belt was stuck. There were only twelve cartridges: two per each of the six weapons captured by Nechipurenko's party, but even this was better than nothing.

Since the bodies of the fallen Nazi soldiers still lay unclaimed about 1 kilometre from the road, Nechipurenko concluded that the German "booty men," and especially the soldiers of the "burial detail" (whose task was to collect the dead), were afraid to venture too far from the road. So Nechipurenko decided to steal up closely to a disabled tank in that area; he was certain that there were weapons in the tank. However, he proved unsuccessful in approaching the tank, for he discovered that the crew and several infantrymen had stayed behind in it. Apparently, the damage was not serious and the tank crew merely waited for assistance in making the repairs.

Even before his encounter with us, Nechipurenko, having hidden his men in the stacks on this side of the shelterbelt, contemplated attacking this tank. To this end, after rejoining our "Sevastopol Battalion," Nechipurenko devised a bold and clever plan which he proposed to Samusev. The Lieutenant asked himself the following question, followed by a reply: "How long does it take to fix an insignificant damage to the engine or the running gear of a tank, a truck or a motorcycle? One day at the most." Yet the Germans had been immobilized for three days, have lit a campfire, and were cooking their meals. This meant that they were waiting for some kind of help to arrive. However, if the vehicle were to be merely towed by a tractor to a repair shop, there was no need for an entire crew to stay behind.

Apparently, an important part or parts were to be delivered, the installation of which would revive the knocked out tank. If this supposition were correct, then a covered transport was bound to arrive shortly with the required parts. This possibility held out much promise to us.

Samusev's and Nechipurenko's groups had been advancing along different routes, yet neither of them saw any traffic controllers or checkpoints along the way. So, we came to the conclusion that our detachment should risk a desperate sally if it were properly armed. After capturing the German truck, in a few hours we could travel a distance that would have taken us days to cover on foot. Before the war, Samusev had been an active member of a motor vehicle club of the *Osoaviakhim* [Society for Assistance to Defence, Aviation, and the Chemical Industry], while Lieutenant Nechipurenko had been a pilot. Both were expert drivers. Admittedly, a group of almost sixty people would not fit into a single truck, no matter how big it was. What about two trips? The more Samusev and Nechipurenko multiplied kilometres by hours, and hours by kilometres, the more the plan seemed attractive to them. One of the soldiers, who had learned by heart the route's reference points on the basis of the information provided by me, was transferred to Nechipurenko's group.

As for Lieutenant Georgiy Nechipurenko, he attached the buckle of his belt to a rusty nail sticking out of the wall and began to sharpen his razor. "What came over you, Zhora? Can't you shave some other time?" Samusev drawled out in disbelief.

"You are missing the point," replied the Lieutenant. "In our squadron we had a middle-aged pilot who had fought in the Spanish Civil War as well as against the Japanese near the Khalkhin-Gol River in Mongolia in 1939. The more difficult a day was expected in his squadron, the more he took pains to look his best. He said it was his belief that good grooming helped you to think. I happen to agree with him."

Nechipurenko took a long time to shave and did a thorough job. When, after washing himself in icy spring water, he finally presented himself to us, Masha and I didn't recognize our tow-haired "policeman." Well-knit, with glistening prominent cheekbones and bushy dark eyebrows, he stood in the centre of the shed slowly rolling the sleeves of his field shirt. Then he carefully wiped the submachine gun handed to him by Samusev, slung it over his right shoulder, slipped a couple of extra cartridge clips into each of his boot tops, smoothed them out with his hands, and put on his field service cap. Then he drew himself up in front of Samusev, and asked him: "Comrade, Senior Lieutenant, may I go?"

"You may." Samusev touched the peak of his creased field service cap. "Good luck to you."

The scouts—Nechipurenko, Zarya, Vasya the homeless orphan, and the sinewy, skinny Serezha Ivanov—filed out of the shed silently. They were instructed to approach the German tank very closely, reconnoitre the approaches to it, and set up an observation post. A decision was made to seize the tank the next morning, so as to allow the rest of us sufficient time to prepare for joining Nechipurenko's small group.

The men spent the rest of the day getting ready in an unhurried fashion, doing peaceful, domestic chores. First they tried to fix their uniforms which had suffered a great deal during our passage through the shelterbelts. Then they washed their footcloths in the spring. Finally, using a piece of porous sandstone to sharpen their knives, they shaved. Meanwhile, Masha and I covered ourselves with our greatcoats and caught a few winks in the corner, snoring quietly. Thus, if you disregarded the sentries who stood guard about 100 metres from our bivouac and changed every hour, you could assume that those gathered in the flimsy shed were not Soviet troops behind enemy lines, but rather some Machine-Tractor Station drivers waiting here for an overdue fellow driver, who was supposed to deliver fuel to the team, but on the way had a drop too much.

As the crimson-red sun rolled down in the blue sky, Samusev kept consulting his watch with ever greater frequency. In a note transmitted by a messenger to Nechipurenko's men, a meeting was set for 2330 hours: we were to come out of the shed with the onset of darkness and start out for the place where the two shelterbelts met at an angle; the messenger of the scouts was to be dispatched there as well. The area was located 4 kilometres from the tank. The distance was beyond the range of aimed fire and, at the same time, made it possible for us to reach either the start lines or cover fairly quickly.

However, by this time Samusev knew that one of his female scouts was almost as blind as a bat in daytime.

We abandoned the shed at 2130 hours, when the first stars spilled out onto the sky, which was still showing blue. When we covered about half of the way, we heard exchange of fire by the road. Our group went to ground and then mounted an advanced guard. The crackle of the sub-machine guns, which alternated with the sound of machine-gun fire, lasted at least 10 minutes, and flares kept going up, one after another. Then, just as unexpectedly, the firing ceased, even though flares continued to mark the night sky at irregular intervals.

Cautiously, one at a time, we arrived at the meeting place, checked out by a patrol member beforehand. Volodya Zarya, the messenger, who was waiting for us there, reported on the situation. He had ascertained that five men watched over the immobilized tank. Apparently feeling uneasy, they took turns in leaving the tank. They returned immediately after relieving themselves. The turret of the tank was pointing toward the forest. The sentry paced in a circle, close to the tank, and was replaced every two hours. One of the tank crew members, apparently the tank commander, armed with both submachine and parabellum guns, walked to the road a few times, and stood there for quite a while, looking expectantly. The distance from the tank to the road was 120-150 metres.

"What was the firing about?" asked Samusev, alarmed.

Zarya sighed. "It started in a stupid way and ended badly. Everything was peaceful before it got dark. We were about to leave when Serega stood up straight. Then and there a flare went up. Apparently, they are so scared they do not economize them. If our idiot had stood up in bushes, they wouldn't have noticed him. Apparently he lost his cool and went to ground with a crash that unnerved them. Fortunately, their sentry showed the direction with his trace inaccurately. The tank machine gun fired from time to time, as if the crew were listening attentively in-between. At first it fired to the right of us, then they traversed the turret and the shots were coming closer and closer. It was fortunate that our

Lieutenant didn't panic; otherwise, we would have all been killed. After all, the vile creature aimed just above the ground, clipping bushes."

"Well, what happened?" interjected Samusev.

"When the machine-gun bursts were coming quite close, Nechipurenko grabbed a healthy-looking branch and threw it to one side, toward the road. He guessed right: a burst was about to end, so it became quiet. Hence, the sentry heard the branch hitting the bushes and let out a trace in that direction, which enabled us to crawl away."

"The three of you?"

"One machine-gun burst reached Ivanov. He was quite far from us. Two bullets hit him in the head and he was killed outright."

"Where is the Lieutenant now?"

"He and Vasya are situated about 300 metres from the tank. He sent you this note."

Samusev covered himself with a raincape, including the head, so as not to give himself away, and struck a match. He hurriedly scanned the crabbed lines of the message, scratched out in the dark. "The Germans are alarmed. Their sentry has to give a password before he is admitted into the tank. A direct attack on our part is out of the question. We must devise a special plan before dawn. I'll continue to observe the tank. Let me know what you intend to do."

By daybreak, a sentry usually becomes less vigilant. He needs to relax after the tension of a nerve-wracking night, when each rustle, each shadow inspires fear in him and might become a harbinger of danger. The coolness of the morning forces him to shiver with the cold, so he has the urge to hide his head as deep as he can in his raised collar; he craves warmth and becomes sleepy. What's more, if at some point earlier he had been scolded for raising a false alarm, he is not inclined to become overly vigilant.

Such was apparently the frame of mind of the sentry who guarded the German tank at dawn on the day we attacked it. During the night the highway was deserted, but then came the first truck, slowing down at the turn by the crossroads. It appeared to stop momentarily and continued on its way. Soon afterwards two "German" soldiers emerged from the shelterbelt into the steppe, crunching dry branches underfoot. Initially ignoring both the tank and the sentry, the soldiers sat down to have something to eat and drink. Then one of the soldiers noticed that the sentry was very interested in their food and bottle. Swallowing hoarsely with his dry throat, the sentry took several steps to one side. The soldier observing the sentry got up, moved away a few paces, and stopped, standing with his legs spread wide apart and a submachine gun slung over his right shoulder. The sentry took a few steps forward, in the direction of the two soldiers, and then and there he stopped, stamping in one spot. Then the soldier who was standing waved at the sentry with a benefactor's gesture, calling him: *"Schnell, Kamrad!"* The sentry came running. In a moment, the soldiers dragged his body, still twitching, into the nearest bushes.

Afterwards, the two men—Volodya Zarya and Aleksey Plotnikov—set off for the tank, barefooted. (The latter had been a pal, as far back as the fighting for Odessa, of Sergey Ivanov who was killed that night.) Plotnikov had a couple of hand grenades attached to his belt, while Zarya was armed with a Schmeisser and carried a German helmet, full of water. Silently striding on the soft, dew-covered grass, the men made their way right up to the target. They listened carefully; it was quiet all around. So Plotnikov climbed onto the tank and Zarya handed him an unusual master-key, a mess tin filled with water. Then Zarya followed Plotnikov onto the tank with his submachine gun at the ready.

Slowly, carefully, and trying to aim exactly into the groove of the closed hatch, Plotnikov began to pour the water Zarya had brought in the helmet. The little stream made a bubbling sound as it penetrated through the hatch. Those in the turret stirred and someone asked a question in German. So Plotnikov's hand shook; a little stream of water missed its target, but it made no difference.

The silence made the click of the bolt seem loud; the cover moved and was raised.... In that instant, Plotnikov, having discarded the helmet, tore with both hands into the rim of the cover, and gave it a violent pull; then and there, Zarya opened up with his submachine gun. Having inserted the barrel into the black hole of the hatch, he didn't take his finger off the trigger until he used up the entire clip. Again there was silence.

At daybreak the movement along the road intensified. A sentry kept walking around the tank, as before, with a submachine gun slung over his shoulder. He wore a heavy helmet and apparently was wounded: the white ring of the bandage covered his chin and extended behind his ears. But the wound couldn't have been serious—the sentry's stride was firm, as was his grip on the barrel of his submachine gun. It was Volodya Zarya. The second "German" soldier was sitting nearby, apparently cooking a meal; he kept throwing branches onto a fire and mixing the boiling contents of a mess tin.

However, the scene has changed somewhat, though the changes would have eluded a superficial inspection. The light machine gun was removed from the tank and stood in the shrubs by the road. Behind it lay Samusev, who had learned in Sevastopol to handle captured weapons expertly. On the other hand, Nechipurenko with six soldiers armed with submachine guns—the cover group—took up a position beside the road. Trucks, motorcycles, and ambulances went by on the road, one after another. None of them paid the slightest attention to the tank, guarded by a sentry as required, or to the sentry himself.

A few hours later, the observers beside the road noticed the approach of a single, slowly crawling covered transport, which stopped before reaching the shelterbelt. An officer stepped out of the cab onto the footboard; he looked around, took out a map, and compared it with the terrain. One of the observers barely raised his hand over the bushes and in that instant another one, situated about 300 metres from the road, noticed a brief flash of a reflected sunbeam. A quiet whistle reached Samusev; he parted the bushes beside him and called out to Zarya, who was taking a stroll around the tank: "It seems they are coming. Get ready!"

After passing the shelterbelt, the vehicle left the road and began to move toward the lone tank. When the indifferently looking sentry, with a chin covered by a bandage, saw the approaching transport, he knocked on the armour of the tank with a stone, and went aside. And when the transport came right up to him, the sentry suddenly noticed something unusual beside the rear wheels. The intrigued driver looked out of the cab. He saw the sentry squatting down beside a rear wheel and carefully picking out a large piece of glass from a broken bottle that was apparently stuck between the tires.

The driver was alarmed; he didn't relish changing a double tire on such a hot day. What's more, he knew that the mowed field could not support a jack. So he jumped out of his cab, rushing toward the sentry. As the driver bent over the wheel, a rough and dirty palm covered his mouth. Subsequently, using a flat bayonet, Zarya knocked him down noiselessly with an accurate blow. Then Zarya pulled himself up, looked into the body of the truck, and saw that there were no enemy soldiers in it.

Zarya experienced a sense of instant relief, for he realized that their plan had almost been carried out; they have captured the tank without any undue noise, and acquired the truck, as well as another complete German uniform. He calmly went around the transport to the other side.

With an obliging gesture, he opened the cab door for the officer, and shot him point-blank in the head.

Then everything happened at lightning speed, as it were. While Samusev, groaning, pulled on the officer's boots with narrow tops, his men ejected tools, boxes, spare parts and welding gas bottles from the body of the truck. Then they jammed four fragmentation hand grenades with their safety pins pulled out between the track shoes of the tank. Plotnikov also placed a hand grenade in the turret, on the shell rack. Using a piece of wire, he joined the grenade's ring to the cover of the upper hatch that was not battened down. After getting out through the driver's peephole, he released the bolt of the hatch cover and firmly slammed the cover shut.

The soldiers scheduled to make the first trip quickly filled the body of the transport, drawing the tarpaulin behind them, while Samusev, looking awkward and strange in his foreign uniform, went around the vehicle, inspecting it in a picky way. Apparently, all was well, so Samusev climbed into the cab and sat down behind the wheel. A soldier with a submachine gun joined him in the cab; it was Plotnikov. Then Zarya climbed into the body of the truck, the telescopic sight mounted on his sniper's rifle.

Samusev noted the operating instructions provided in the cab by the manufacturer of the truck: a gear shift diagram engraved on the plastic head of the gear box lever and an illustration showing the starting handle beside the starter key. Then he started the engine, backed up the heavy three-axle transport, turned, and drove the vehicle toward the road. Left behind to lead the group scheduled to make the second trip, Nechipurenko ran up to the truck after it had stopped beside the road. He jumped onto the footboard, firmly squeezed the outstretched hand of Samusev, and questioningly looked into his grey, narrow-shaped, hawk-like eyes. Samusev reassured him. "Don't worry, Zhora, everything will turn out according to our plan. The ride should take no more than three hours, and we'll immediately come back to get you. I'll leave the girls with you; I believe this would be less risky. Take cover. Judging by the map, it would be possible for you to hide to the south of here as well, where there are forested areas without large Cossack villages. Begin sending signals to the road in about five hours."

"Yes, Sir!" Nechipurenko forced himself to look away. "Don't worry, commander! You should be the first to go. After all, we are not staying behind unarmed. We've seven submachine guns and one machine gun, and there is one hand grenade for everyone. The Nazis would not be able to capture us now!"

"All right, Zhora," ended Samusev, inappropriately. "If I survive, I'll definitely come back, but if fate decides otherwise I am sure you'll know what to do...." Instead of replying, Nechipurenko firmly squeezed Samusev's broad hand until it hurt and jumped off the footboard. The huge transport started with a jerk; quickly accelerating, it raised a lot of dust.

Samusev realized that the Germans had breached the front in a very important sector; they were strong, well-fed, impudent, and bent on gaining access to the Caucasian oil. He knew that his group needed the most improbable piece of luck, the rarest coincidence of favourable events to evade all the misadventures that were likely to befall them, for the probability of such misadventures occurring was much greater than of even the slightest success. Yet, in spite of all the odds against us, he —Senior Lieutenant Samusev—was sitting behind the steering wheel of a powerful and obedient enemy vehicle. Together with his comrades, he was behaving as a master in his own house, though operating on an enemy-occupied territory. So he was filled with reckless, boyish joy.

Meanwhile, his soldiers stood huddled together in the body of the truck, holding on to the arcs of the iron supports. Two of them standing in the front have pierced the tarpaulin roof with their knives and carefully examined the road ahead of them through the holes, while those at the back observed the disappearing ribbon of the highway just as attentively. Their arms at the ready, the soldiers were prepared to deal calmly with even the most unexpected situations.

In two hours Samusev's group covered 56 kilometres. Then they orientated themselves beside a small bridge across a deep ravine. Judging by the map taken from the killed officer, the nearest Cossack village was 8 kilometres away. Samusev turned left, and quickly drove the Daimler truck along a level meadow, away from the road. His intuition prompted him to seek an appropriate shelter in that direction. In fact, after covering 4 kilometres, he reached thick shrubs growing along the edge of a ravine. He decided that its sloping banks would make it possible to drive the vehicle down into the ravine and to camouflage it very well. Samusev left Zarya in charge and immediately went back to get us.

On the way, he even made a detour to the closest melon field, where he purchased about thirty excellent, ripe water melons, which he threw into the body of the truck. Admittedly, the old man who was guarding the melon field did not share Samusev's jubilant mood and acted a role that was somewhat out of keeping with Samusev's scheme of things. With a scowl on his face he sucked on an empty pipe and diplomatically pretended not to notice that the "German" officer and soldier had selected the biggest and best melons. To make up for it, the old man displayed a remarkable burst of energy and eloquence when the "Nazis" thanked him. In reply to the Russian form of address "grandfather," the watchman dished out to them such a multitude of ingenious old Cossack curses—wishing them, their parents, their children, and their grand-children that they come down with so many awful ailments—that Samusev hastily returned to the truck.

Subsequently, they twice encountered motor transport columns going in the opposite direction, but no one paid attention to the lone truck. During such encounters Samusev kept his vehicle close to the shoulder of the road. He accelerated then as much as he could, blowing his horn continuously. The kindly Kuban' dust added an excellent final touch to the camouflage.

The meeting with Nechipurenko and his group took place at the agreed time and place, behind a narrow clearing through which passed a sloping sideroad that joined the highway to a country road. There, the thick wall of foliage concealed the vehicle only a few dozens of metres from the highway.

Using the fuel in the iron drum left in the truck body beforehand, we topped up the fuel tank, checked the tires, and inspected the engine oil level. Afterwards, we tossed several sheaves onto the floor of the truck body at the back, and placed our choice water melons on them in three rows. Then everyone, including Nechipurenko, climbed into the body of the truck. Though we were ready to go, for some reason Samusev was taking his time. Therefore, Nechipurenko lifted the tarpaulin and bent forward to talk to the driver.

"Are you, by any chance, waiting for the Germans?" he asked.

"You guessed it right," replied Samusev, casting a sidelong glance at him; there was mischief in his merry eyes.

"Are you crazy?" demanded Nechipurenko.

"Not in the least!" replied Samusev.

"You got the urge to play with fire?" again demanded Nechipurenko.

"With smoke," said Samusev roaring with laughter. He then lowered his voice and continued: "You know we've managed to get here on the sly, but what's going to happen to us on the way back? Suppose someone succeeds in catching up with us, someone ahead waits for us, and someone gets curious. The result would be a lot of noise and an exchange of fire.... We would be finished."

"Well, what have you got in mind?"

"We ought to join a motor vehicle column. We should let it pass and then stay with it, bringing up the rear. Behind the dust, like behind a smoke screen, not a devil himself would notice us. Again, if there is a checkpoint, they'll inspect the papers of the forward vehicle. The longer the column, the better!"

"We are risking a great deal," Nechipurenko offered doubtfully. "We are putting ourselves in their clutches...."

"That's it! You think what we are doing is a crazy idea, but it would never occur to them. We are taking a well-calculated risk."

"Suppose we run into a German security detachment?" asked Nechipurenko, still unconvinced.

"It's not likely. The front is quite far to the east and the terrain is open, inappropriate for guerilla warfare, so they are not afraid. As for the patrolmen on motorcycles, Plotnikov will hear them; after all, he is sitting in the cab beside a window. Everything will turn out as planned, Zhorik; don't worry. We'll yet reach friendly troops, galloping on this 'elephant.'"

Even a most risky plan, such as ours was, doesn't necessarily have to be difficult to carry out, and in fact Samusev's expectations eventually proved to be entirely correct. Meanwhile, for the soldiers hiding in the truck body this journey was very taxing. It was difficult to maintain your composure while sitting under the dark tarpaulin a hundred paces away from the enemy; you involuntarily held your breath each time you became aware of the gears being shifted and each time you heard the brakes squeal. But to make up for it, in three and a half hours the "expedition" successfully reached the small wooden bridge which was our reference point.

As soon as the truck stopped, Plotnikov immediately jumped out of the cab. Holding a bucket, he scrambled to the bottom of the deep ravine under the bridge. And should one of the Germans riding at the end of the column, now rapidly disappearing from view, happened to turn around at that moment, he would have seen a routine road scene: a truck with a raised hood and a soldier pouring water into the radiator. Admittedly, Plotnikov had to make several trips to the bottom of the ravine, to ensure that the column moved away as far as possible. However, he was so excited that he didn't even feel tired from making all these trips.

Then we again turned aside, and soon the transport slowly backed into the ravine. Our two groups were now reunited.

* * *

In choosing a shelter for our next thirty-six hour halt, Samusev was motivated by two considerations. First of all, he found it necessary to estimate our situation again, for our group was approaching heavily populated localities in Stavropol Territory. In addition, his subordinates at the very least needed a short rest. Exhausted by constant nervous tension, lengthy marching, and hunger, as well as suffering from lack of sleep, we were literally all dropping from fatigue.

Also, we were quite hard-up in terms of our food supply; our individual daily rations consisted of a water melon, corn cooked over the hot flame obtained from burning the tall weeds, a couple of slices of bread, and a piece of lard the size of a matchbox. So Samusev devised a special plan to obtain the necessary food supplies for us.

Our sniper Volodya Zarya happened to be a native of Stavropol Territory we were crossing, and occasionally visited his relatives in this area. Though Zarya had not been here for some time, Samusev intended to ask him for his help in making contact with the local population. When Zarya first saw the small bridge thrown over the ravine, he thought it looked familiar, so he decided to try his luck in locating the village of Podgor'ye in which his grandmother lived. Without waiting for Samusev's return, he sent two soldiers to reconnoitre the area. They had not come back by the time we arrived, so Zarya decided to set off for the village himself and I was to accompany him.

By the time we left in the late afternoon, dark clouds moved in and it began to rain. At first sparse and indecisive, as it were, the rain gradually intensified. When Zarya and I, as well as the three soldiers covering us, reached the village meadow, it was pouring continuously. The strong gusts of wind grabbed the small, frequent rain drops, and turned them into a fine spray. It was difficult to see anything behind this curtain of rain, so a small shepherd boy, who had covered his head and shoulders with a sack made of matting that was folded in half to form a kind of a hood, didn't notice me until I came right up to him.

I found out from him that there were no Germans in the village. And then the unexpected happened. When Zarya, wearing a German rain-cape and at first observing our encounter from a distance, approached us closer, he recognized the little shepherd boy. It was Pet'ka Shkodar' who lived three houses away from Zarya's grandmother Ul'ya.

Blue from the cold and clenching his teeth so that the multitude of freckles stood out prominently on his cheekbones, the shepherd boy silently grabbed a whip. Then, after smacking the nearest cow several times, he began to run away from us. Truly upset, Zarya threw up his hands. "What a misfortune! Our intelligence has vanished. We'll have to explore the village blindly," he said.

"Would it be worthwhile, Volodya?" I asked.

"What else is there to do? We have not reconnoitred the area. As to grub, we don't know the prospects for obtaining it, either. Also, I must tell you I fear for my grandmother. This Shkodar' will drag my name in the mud in the entire village; if this happens, the old woman would not be able to live it down. Anyway, let's go and face the music; we can't hide now," replied Zarya.

His prognosis proved to be quite accurate. By the time we approached his grandmother's gate, which was hanging on home-made loops fashioned from a driving belt, a group of animatedly chattering women neighbours had already gathered by the cottage fence. Neither the rain nor the cold wind impeded them from patiently waiting at the crossroads for the grandson of grandmother Ul'yana. The expressions on the women's faces were so eloquent that when Zarya passed them he involuntarily felt the butt of the submachine gun under his raincape.

Ul'yana Andreyevna met us on the threshold. The withered, thin old woman held a big, heavy poker, which she had grabbed with the intent of using as an improvised weapon. "What a rotten egg!" she exclaimed. "Presented himself and even dragged in his companion! Chase him away, my good people!" And Ul'yana Andreyevna raised the poker, advancing toward her grandson. Even though the situation had its comical side, Zarya and I had not the slightest desire to laugh. How was he to mollify the angry old woman? Besides, the neighbours who had gathered behind the fence could have come to her aid at any moment.

However, one must not assume that the female members of the village population were always reckless in opposing any member of the army of occupation. Undoubtedly, the women would not have been as pugnacious if in Zarya's place they encountered a real German, or even a Russian stranger employed by the Germans, say as policeman. To the villagers, any other male in the foreign uniform would have seemed totally mysterious and incomprehensible, and therefore doubly dangerous. On the other hand, none of the women could simply acknowledge in Vovka Zarya, whom the majority of them knew as a child, a full-fledged member of the army of occupation. Admittedly, the village women considered him a traitor worthy of universal contempt; yet, at the same time, they treated him almost as a relative and thus one not to be feared in the least.

It is difficult to say how the messy situation would have ended if I haven't come up with a good idea. From my bosom I pulled out my creased field service cap with a crimson star, and rushed toward Ul'yana Andreyevna, extending to her the cap as my identification or credentials: "Here, look!"

Even though at this time anyone who went beyond the village outskirts could have easily obtained all kinds of uniforms—and often weapons of both armies as well—the field service cap with a little red star proved effective in calming down the aroused passions. So Ul'yana Andreyevna dropped the poker; having lowered herself onto her front steps, she began to cry quietly, in a manner of old people.

However, the women neighbours, who had not yet fully understood the situation but were already quite calm, moved away from the fence and engaged in a quiet discussion.

Then we both entered Zarya's grandmother's cottage. Having collected himself, Zarya took off his German uniform to dry it out, retaining only his shirt. As for me, I quickly changed into a dry dress of the mistress of the house and made myself comfortable by the stove, trying to warm up my chilled body.

Suddenly, we heard a hoarse yet loud voice behind the front door. "May I come in, Ul'yana Andreyevna?"

"Come in, come in, Mefod'yevich," replied the old woman and turned to her grandson to reassure him: "This is Trofim Mefod'yevich, our team leader."

An elderly Cossack, still strong like an ox, entered the cottage, shaking off the raindrops from his splendid forked beard. But for the empty sleeve attached with a safety pin to his right shoulder, even the strictest medical board would have found him fit for active service. There was not a single grey hair in his beard or head of brown hair; his teeth were even and white like lumps of sugar; and under his confident steps the floor boards creaked and bent. Only the thick net of wrinkles, furrowing his brick-coloured face, tanned by the steppe sun, as well as his hoarse voice, betrayed his advanced age.

After exchanging the usual greetings, the team leader approached the kitchen table and lowered himself onto a bench. "I see you've visitors, Ul'yana Andreyevna. Have they come from afar?"

"We happen to be paying a neighbourly visit...." replied Zarya in a somewhat rude manner, giving the stranger a guarded look.

"And where are you going?"

"Have you heard about the Kudykina Mountain, Father?" Zarya inquired sarcastically.

Looking angry, Trofim Mefod'yevich abruptly got up from the bench. His kindly but cunning face immediately became heavier and his speech lost its Ukrainian melodiousness, becoming disjointed and chopped. "You're silly, lad. Who are you trying to kid? I am in my seventh decade. I've lived through three wars; and I was awarded both the Cross of St. George and the Order of the Red Banner. I see right through smart alecks like yourself. Don't you realize this? You came to reconnoitre your route. Don't waste time and say what's on your mind. No one can give you directions better than I." Then he sat down again, pulling out a very long tobacco pouch from the pocket of his pants.

Trofim Mefod'yevich turned out to be a veritable gold mine of information. The only person in the village to own a radio, a crystal receiver—which didn't have to be plugged into an electrical circuit and required no batteries to operate—he regularly listened to the communiqués of *Sovinformburo*, and had excellent knowledge of the situation in the area that he knew inside out. We learned that the front had moved far to the south; the Germans had already occupied Armavir and came right up to Mozdok. He told us to march to Kizlyar, to the sandy steppes of Groznyy Region.

"There is not enough soldiers in any army to maintain uninterrupted front lines there. Of course, there will be reconnaissance patrols, and you'll encounter garrisons; nevertheless, if you must break out, do it only there. How many are there in your party?"

"Let's see: less than a company and more than a platoon," I replied, provoking a reproachful look on the part of Zarya. By then I trusted Trofim Mefod'yevich completely and didn't consider it necessary to be overly secretive in his presence. The old man became pensive for a moment. After moving out of the way the bowls and glasses that Ul'yana Andreyevna had already put on the table, he drew on its surface a wavy line with the sharp end of his flint and steel for striking a spark. "Look. Here is the river. I don't know its official name on the map, but the Cossacks call it Solonitsa. It's shallow and in the fall one can ford it. Get a supply of water there and turn to the right. Your trip would be difficult; there are no wells and no lakes, but the Nazis are not likely to be there, either. In four days you'll reach the Kalmyk country. Did you memorize all of this?"

"Yes, Sir!" replied Zarya, as behoved one junior in rank.

Neither we, the scouts, nor the team leader had the time for a lengthy visit. The hands of my watch, which I kept consulting, reminded us that we had a long way to go to the road, that the three soldiers of the cover group were getting wet in the rain, and that our detachment was impatiently awaiting the news we were expected to bring.

We emptied a glass of home-brew each, and ate a plateful of scrambled eggs, with lard, potatoes and sour milk. Trofim Mefod'yevich was not averse to having another glass of the home-brew, but Zarya, who was sensing how alcohol immediately went to his head—the three hungry days told on him—got up from the table resolutely.

However, Ul'yana Andreyevna intervened then and there: "What about me?"

"Grandmother Ul'ya," said Zarya reproachfully, "I am a soldier; my place...."

"I know your place, only how can I face them? I want them to know you're not a traitor. I can't visit every cottage and keep on proving it to everyone, over and over again."

"All right, Grandmother Ul'ya, we'll think up something," Zarya hastened to reassure her, even though he was not quite sure what to do. However, fate itself intervened!

Trofim Mefod'yevich, having emptied one more goblet of the home-brew before leaving, went to see us off. The alcohol had apparently affected the old Cossack—he was so talkative on the way. We learned from him that his village team had hidden their grain and fuel, needed to sow the spring crops; and the "women's battalion" of the Machine-Tractor Station had even managed to bring a tractor to an old threshing floor, which they had thoroughly concealed with straw.

We said good-bye. On parting, we didn't know that we'll meet again soon. We got lost in the dark and wandered about the steppe for several hours. By the time we approached our bivouac, squelching with our boots on the soft ground and frequently slipping, it was just before dawn and the rain had stopped. Still at a distance from the ravine—about several hundred metres away—we heard the strained and choking hum of a motor vehicle engine, so we understood that something unexpected had happened.

While selecting the site for a halt, Samusev neglected to take into account a likely change in the weather. To conceal the heavy Daimler, he drove it to the bottom of the ravine. Then the rain, growing more and more intensive, sent thousands of tiny streams running down the slopes. By the time anyone realized what was happening, the rear axle of the truck was stuck in the soft earth almost right up to the differential and the vehicle was trapped.

The men struggled for several hours, under the torrential rain, to free the truck. Had the weather been different or if we had a rope, fifty people could have freed the transport quite easily. With the men's boots slipping in the mud, the Daimler refused to give way. Admittedly, having thrown heaps of hazel twigs under the wheels as well as greatcoats and raincoats, in the end they managed to pull the vehicle out of its clayish trap, but it could not climb the slope. It kept skidding and rolling back, so it was lucky that no one was injured. However, our worst problem was shortage of fuel; we used up almost all of it. The tank was not more than a quarter full, and the drum had been empty since the day earlier.

After Zarya reported to Samusev, the latter calmed down somewhat. Fate seemed to favour us, after all. Our group took off their uniforms, wrung them out, and kept jumping up and down in an attempt to warm themselves up in the rays of the rising sun. Samusev and Nechipurenko were less chilled than the others, because they spent several hours taking turns at the wheel in the cab, where it was not only dry but warm as well, each of them hoping he would be the lucky one to get the vehicle out of the ravine.

"Well, what should we do next, Lieutenant?" asked Samusev, staring at Georgiy Nechipurenko. "Should we abandon the truck and make our way on foot? We have a long way to go."

"Indeed! Three hundred kilometres.... We'll have a hard time without the truck. Perhaps it will dry up a little in three hours, since there is not a cloud in the sky. Only we won't be able to get very far on this supply of fuel."

"Comrade Senior Lieutenant!" exclaimed Zarya standing on the footboard. "I'll get you at least one drum of fuel," he said excitedly.

"Are you going to give birth to it?" asked Nechipurenko sarcastically. "You've a sense of humour, Senior Sergeant, but we're not in a mood for jokes."

However, Zarya, delighted by the idea that had unexpectedly ocurred to him, was not offended. "Cut it out!" he reacted. "I am completely serious. Our collective farm workers will share their fuel with us—I know for sure that they have hidden some gasoline. Only...."

"Only what?" Samusev interrupted him impatiently, still unconvinced as well.

"I haven't told you about the reception I was given in the village. Well, I was sort of ashamed. Of course, Mefod'yevich can be trusted, but he is not the only one to have a say and I am not sure about the women.

Trofim Mefod'yevich told us that when our troops were retreating through the village, the Cossack women had cursed them terribly. The troops' retreat distressed them a great deal...."

"It distressed them, you say?" Samusev repeated thoughtfully. Turning sharply toward Nechipurenko, he added: "Listen to me, Zhora. Suppose, we..."

So Masha and I went to the village later on that morning, met with Trofim Mefod'yevich, and reached an understanding about sharing the villagers' fuel with us.

A few hours later, the Daimler made it to the village meadow on its final litres of gasoline, and stopped beside a large stack. From the truck emerged two well-armed groups of soldiers of the "platoon on parade," who had spared no effort to look their best. They bypassed Podgor'ye on both sides and then, starting simultaneously at the opposite ends of its main street, entered the village. And the sound of their solemn and stately song floated, as it were, over the cottages of the village:

> Rise, our huge country,
> Rise to fight to the death....

All the inhabitants of Podgor'ye couldn't help but come out of their cottages at this moment. The sorrowful and powerful melody, known to everyone, pealed like an alarm bell, breaking the morning silence. Marching in step, the column kept advancing along the main street. To one side proudly marched Volodya Zarya, his rifle with a telescopic sight slung over right shoulder and the ruby-red Order of the Red Star shining on his chest.

And even though the war had completely weaned us of sentimentality, and we were hungry and weakened, we considered ourselves then as special representatives of our nation on this enemy-occupied, though not conquered land. And what we experienced then was so intense that you felt a lump forming in your throat.

What we did then was completely devoid of any practical purpose. Yet behind the fact that here, on enemy-held territory, our soldiers improvised a parade, was a higher purpose that was impossible to express verbally but was understood by each and everyone of us. The improvised parade filled a need, both for the soldiers who marched in their worn boots along the muddy village street—which had not yet dried out after the rain—and the villagers who, filled with faith and hope, were observing the odd spectacle we had staged.

Five days earlier, we, a group of patients discharged from various hospitals, found ourselves behind enemy lines. Our first encounter with the enemy turned us back into soldiers. Marching on the improvised parade, we felt as if we were victors, and each and everyone of us understood that this sensation will leave a permanent imprint on our lives.

On the other hand, those who looked at us from the sidelines; those who ran ahead of our formation, neglecting to wipe off their tears of joy; and those who dashed to their hiding-places to give away the last bit of stashed-away foodstuffs—what did these people feel? Even though their joy was short-lived, it was nevertheless a moment of great faith in the future, for the sake of which it was worthwhile to live and struggle....

After six days of wandering across Nazi-occupied territory in the captured Daimler, our "Sevastopol Battalion" reached friendly troops in the vicinity of Kizlyar.

CONCLUSION

Immediately after the soldiers of the "Sevastopol Battalion" broke out of their encirclement, they were assigned to various military units. As for me, after graduating from a course for junior lieutenants, I served as commander of an air defence machine-gun platoon, commander of a machine-gun platoon, and finally commander of a machine-gun company. Eventually, I reached the rank of senior lieutenant. I stayed in the army on active service until the fall of 1944. Even though much earlier a medical board had certified me as being only conditionally fit for military service, and for a time I stayed with a reserve regiment in Khar'kov, I succeeded in persuading my superiors to send me back to the front. I was to accompany a reserve company to the battle zone.

However, we never reached our destination. As a result of an air raid on the way, I sustained a severe concussion and became an invalid. In time, after the defeat of Nazi Germany, I regained some vision, and in a few years I was even able to write. I am still interested in the history of my famous unit, and have not forgotten my promise given to Nina Onilova in the spring of 1942 that, were I to survive, I would tell the story of my comrades-in-arms of the Chapayev Division who were so dear to me; I would write about their feats of arms during the defence of Odessa and Sevastopol, the famous stronghold on the Black Sea.

I was fortunate to have been able to attend a recent reunion of the participants in the defence of Sevastopol, which took place on its twenty-fifth anniversary. On this occasion, my fellow veterans and I visited the sites of former battles. We became re-acquainted with the dazzlingly beautiful city, raised from ruins. I had never been in Sevastopol before the war. I saw it for the first time a quarter of a century ago on a cloudy December day, before it was stormed by Nazi troops. It was then a fighting city, which had withstood several trials by fire, a city of destroyed streets, of gaping wounds.

They say that Sevastopol was exceptionally beautiful before the war. However, it looks truly fabulous now. And if those who had fallen defending the city could have seen it as it presented itself to us, they undoubtedly would have been gratified that their blood had not been spilled in vain. Moreover, it had been a very emotional experience for us to learn that those who fell here have not been forgotten, and their memory is cherished.

We admired the resurrected Sevastopol, reminiscing about our com-rades-in-arms. The distant past rose forcefully before the mind's eye. It was here, on the former tactical line, where a young forest rustles again, that sniper Volodya Zarya and scout Vasya Kozhevnikov carried out their missions. Here, during a battle, they rescued Senior Lieutenant Ivan Samusev.

Here was permanent strong point No. 1 of Morozov's platoon. From this pillbox I delivered fire, containing the Nazi onslaught during the dif-ficult days of the June storm.

In June, our regimental HQ was located somewhere on this slope. From here, Major Antipin, commanding officer of our regiment, went into a desperate attack together with the remnants of the HQ defence pla-toon. Not too far from this site, Colonel Neustroyev, our divisional chief of staff, was wounded during an air raid; it was my meeting with him in the hospital in Sochi that had determined my military career.

Only a handful of veterans of the Chapayev Division were able to come to our veterans' reunion. A soldier is vulnerable; every war claims its victims. All the same, I wanted to believe that there were some who couldn't come because of an urgent business, or because an invitation to the reunion had failed to reach them. At the reunion, I recognized only the odd veteran from among those I knew during those distant and tragic years; I met the majority of the participants for the first time. However, as a result of the reunion, I was able to establish contact with twenty veterans of the Chapayev Division. Here is information about some of the defenders of Sevastopol:

Our lively divisional commanding officer, Lieutenant-General Trofim Kalinovich Kolomiyets, is still full of energy. After he recovered from the concussion sustained on 30 June 1942 in Sevastopol, Trofim Kalinovich was appointed deputy commanding officer of the 51st Army. Subse-sequently, he commanded the 54th Rifle Corps, which took part in the liberation of Sevastopol. He finished his wartime service in the capacity of deputy commanding officer of the 2nd Guards Army. Our general survived two serious wounds and three severe concussions. Though he retired a long time ago, he still devotes a great deal of his time and effort to lecturing about the war before young people in Volgograd, where he resides.

Colonel (Retired) Parfentiy Grigor'yevich Neustroyev, chief of staff of our Chapayev Division, after leaving the hospital became commandant of the Infantry School in Orel. Subsequently, he was appointed Regional Military Commissar [recruitment officer] of Omsk and stayed in that city after he retired.

Colonel Nikolay Vasil'yevich Zakharov, the first commanding officer of our 287th Rifle Regiment and a favourite of Chapayev troops, was killed in Sevastopol in June 1942. On the other hand, Major Mikhail Stepanovich Antipin, who had replaced Zakharov, ended the war in Königsberg in the capacity of deputy commanding officer of a motor rifle brigade. He served in the army until very recently and retired not too long ago in the rank of Colonel, due to poor health. I was terribly sorry to learn the details of Major Boris Anisimovich Shestopalov's death. He had been our regimental chief of staff and then suceeded Major Antipin as commanding officer of our regiment. A few days before the end of Sevastopol's defence he was badly wounded and blew himself up with a hand grenade....

However, Kondrat Vasil'yevich Kutsenko, former chief of our regimental combat engineers, is alive and well. Many years ago, he secured employment in a Tula area mine and is now a mine sector chief in the town of Sokol'niki. Regrettably, I have completely lost track of Pavel Andreyevich Morozov, commander of our machine-gun platoon and my dear mentor and teacher. I learned that he had been severely wounded in the vicinity of Khersones Lighthouse. He was taken prisoner, but in captivity also behaved like a true patriot and an honourable soldier. Finally, Sergey Ivanovich Zudin, former chief of logistics of our regiment, keeps well and is the manager of a large establishment in Moscow.

Both happy and sad, I said good-bye to the city which had become so dear to me still during the war. Our encounters resembled meetings between old friends whose friendship endures in spite of their separation. There, in Sevastopol, a part of my difficult, but nevertheless wonderful youth had been left behind forever. There were people near me whom I respected and loved with all my heart, and whom I'll never forget. And, when we recall those whom we loved, to us they seem eternally alive. So, among those who will live in my memory forever are Vanya Samusev, Volodya Miroshnichenko, Vasya Kozhevnikov, Masha Ivanova, Andryushka Zaytsev, Nina Onilova, Kolya Sizov, Tolya Samarskiy, Olya and Fedya Tkachenko and Volodya Zarya.

Nina Andreyevna ONILOVA

THE DEATH OF NINA ONILOVA

A. Khamadan, a Soviet writer, describes Nina Onilova's final moments thus:

"She was lying in a cave with a high ceiling, hollowed out in rock. An electric bulb, covered with gauze, emitted a soft light. A nurse sat at the foot of the bed.

"'Sometimes she opens her eyes,' whispered Varshavskiy, chief of the medical division. 'She says two-three words and again sinks into a semi-conscious state. We are doing everything modern medicine is capable of, but she has been wounded too many times and has lost too much blood. Only miracle can save her. But...'

"He pronounced the word 'but' so mercilessly!

"Nina Onilova faded away in silence. She opened her eyes, looked at us, and didn't recognize us. She then shifted her gaze to the light of the bulb and looked at it for a long time without blinking her eyes. Varshavskiy abruptly pulled the gauze off the bulb. The bright light splashed into her eyes, but she didn't take them off the light. On the contrary, she seemed to peer at it even more intently, as if trying to memorize its brightness. Varshavskiy replaced the gauze on the bulb. Onilova lowered her eyelids and immediately raised them. Varshavskiy bent toward her ear and asked:

"'Do you wish to say something?'

"Onilova again glanced at the bulb.

"'Does the light bother you?' again asked Varshavskiy.

"She lowered her eyelids, and shook her head almost imperceptibly. We understood that the light didn't bother her.

"'Do you want anything?' Varshavskiy persevered.

"But she kept looking at the light. Finally, we noticed a bundle of papers lying on the table under the light. Varshavskiy picked it up; Onilova smiled and whispered something inaudibly. We opened the bundle. It contained *Sevastopolskiye rasskazy* [Sevastopol Stories] by L. Tolstoy, a student's exercise book, a bundle of letters addressed to Onilova...and clippings from military newspapers, describing her exploits.

"We opened the exercise book. The first few pages were filled with

Onilova's hasty, illegible handwriting. She had copied in full the text of the Maritime Army's song 'The Sea Spread Over a Wide Area Beside Our Native Crimean Shores.' On the second page, there was an unfinished letter addressed 'To the real Anka the Machine Gunner from the Chapayev Division, whom I saw in the film *Chapayev*.' [The film star who played the role of the Civil War heroine.]

"Apparently she had carefully read Tolstoy's book about Sevastopol, underlining in pencil a number of words and lines excerpted from the book; her exclamation signs, and sometimes brief comments as well, appeared in the margins:

"'That's correct!'

"'How true!'

"'I felt the same way!'

"'Fighting comes very easily to you, if you don't think about dying. You must understand why you are risking your life. If you seek glory for its own sake, that's very bad. Only those exploits are commendable that are inspired by love for one's people and country. Keep in mind that you are defending yourself and your country; heroism and glory will then come to you of their own accord.'

"The stubborn, frantic struggle to save the life of this very nice young girl went on. Battalions, regiments, and divisions kept inquiring every five to ten minutes about the condition of the brave machine gunner. Everyone was anxious and concerned about Nina. But the replies were not very comforting. Finally, Lida, the nurse on duty beside the telephone, exclaimed in desperation:

"'I can't stand it any longer! People want to hear that she is getting better, so I am bound to upset them. I must tell them that Nina's condition is rapidly deteriorating!'

"The army commander stood in the hospital room, bending over Onilova's bed. His head twitching, he looked Onilova straight in the eye, with a kindly, fatherly smile. She responded by gazing at him just as intently. The general lowered himself heavily onto a chair, placed his hand on Onilova's forehead, and stroked her hair. The shadow of a grateful smile appeared on her lips.

"'Well, little daughter, you fought gloriously,' he said in a slightly hoarse voice. 'Thank you on behalf of our entire army and our entire nation.... Everyone in Sevastopol knows about you. The entire country will learn about you, too. Thank you, little daughter....'"[7]

ENDNOTES

1. See, for instance, my "Soviet Women in Combat in World War II: The Rear Services, Resistance Behind Enemy Lines and Military Political Workers," *International Journal of Women's Studies*, Vol. 5, No. 4 (September/October 1982), pp. 364-65.

2. Z.M.Medvedeva, "Zapiski pulemetchitsy [Notes of a Machine-Gunner]," *Don*, Nos. 3 and 4 (1971), pp. 147-66, 140-51; continued in *Don*, Nos. 1 and 2 (1975), pp. 165-74, 129-50. See also "Otvazhnaya pulemetchitsa [A Brave Woman Machine Gunner]," in N.I. Karayev and V.V.Lyubimov, eds., *Nam dorogi eti pozabyt' nel'zya* [We Must Not Forget] (Rostov-na-Donu: Knizhnoye izdatel'stvo: 1975), pp. 44-52.

3. Z.M. Medvedeva, "Iz dnevnika voyennykh let [From My War Diary]," in P.Ye. Garmash, ed. *Za rodnoy Sevastopol* [For Our Own Sevastopol]. 2nd rev. ed. (Moscow: Molodaya Gvardiya, 1983), p. 132.

4. "Chapayevtsy stoyali na smert' [Soldiers of the Chapayev Division Stood to the Last Man]," in *U chernomorskikh tverdyn'* [At the Black Sea Strong-holds] (Moscow: Voyenizdat, 1967), pp. 216-17.

5. *Inkerman Caves*: a former stronghold of the ancient Dorians, hewed out in rock in the Crimea and known under the Greek name of *Kalamita* until the fifteen century A.D., at which time it was renamed *Inkerman* by the Turks. During the Crimean War (1853-56), it was the site of the famous Inkerman Battle, which took place on 24 October 1854. See *Bol'shaya Sovetskaya Entsiklopediya* [The Great Soviet Encyclopedia], 2nd ed., XVIII, 163.

6. *Khersones Lighthouse:* This lighthouse of World War II fame stood in the vicinity of the ancient Greek town of Chersonesus, situated on a peninsula 3 miles west of Sevastopol. Chersonese (Chersonesus or Cherronesus) denotes "peninsula" in ancient geography, with Tauric Chersonese referring to the entire Crimean Peninsula. See *Encyclopaedia Britannica*, 1964 ed., V, 452; *Bol'shaya Sovetskaya Entsiklopediya* [The Great Soviet Encyclopedia], 2nd. ed., XXXXVI, 122-23.

7. *Sevastopol'tsy* [Defenders of Sevastopol] (Moscow: Molodaya Gvardiya, 1942), p. 10, cited in G.I. Vaneyev, *Geroini Sevastopol'skoy kreposti* [Heroines of the Sevastopol Stronghold] (Simferopol: Krym, 1965), pp. 92-93.

SCHEDULED TO APPEAR IN 1997/1998

WOMEN IN AIR WAR:
THE EASTERN FRONT OF WORLD WAR II
Ed. and trans. by Kazimiera J. Cottam
(Memoirs of Soviet airwomen who served in three women's regiments.)

DEFENDING LENINGRAD:
WOMEN BEHIND ENEMY LINES
Ed. and trans. by Kazimiera J. Cottam
(The story of two partisans and one secret agent.)

WOMEN IN WAR AND RESISTANCE:
SELECTED BIOGRAPHIES OF SOVIET WOMEN SOLDIERS
by Kazimiera J. Cottam

(A collection consisting of 100 original mini-biographies. Includes thirty-five biographies of bomber, fighter, and ground attack pilots and navigators, and one radio-operator/air gunner, in addition to other military personnel, partisans and secret agents.)